RawSome Recipes

Mostly RAW
with SOME cooked...

whole foods for vital nutrition!

Robyn Boyd

Photographs by Lynn Wagner

Photo: Thai Appetizer (page 123)

Important Disclaimer

The information in this book is intended to be informative and in no way used as a diagnosis or prescription. When changing your diet or exercise regime, it is always suggested that you seek appropriate wise counsel from your doctor or health care professional. The author, publisher, and distributors of this book are not responsible for any changes in your body as a result of your choice to implement anything suggested in writing within the contents of these pages.

The intention of these recipes is to inspire you to make healthy choices, to encourage you to enjoy the art and delight of healthful food preparation, and to educate you about the tremendous benefits of eating the foods God has given us to keep us vital.

We encourage you to make and share these recipes and the joy of "uncooking" with all your friends and family! Eat well and be well!

Second Edition

©Copyright July 2004 Robyn Boyd

ISBN 0-943685-41-9

Printed in the United States of America   10 9 8 7 6 5 4 3 2 1

Published and Distributed by Essential Science Publishing
To order additional copies of this book call (800)336-6308 or visit us on the web at www.essentialscience.net

Cover Photographs:

Top to bottom:	*Recipe on page:*
Fresh Almond Milk	*59*
RawSome Hummus Dip (shown with red & yellow bell peppers)	*130*
Santa Cruz Solar Tacos	*68*
Spa Salad	*82*
Raw Fruit Tart	*146*
RawSome Apricot & Peach Cobbler	*143*

Acknowledgments

I dedicate this book first and foremost to God, because without Him as my compass and light on the journey of life, I am lost.

To my husband Rennie and daughter Molly, who are so supportive of my "uncooking" and many recipe trial and errors.

To my Mom who has always supported me in my ventures and who so efficiently and faithfully helped me with many aspects of this book.

To my friends who so enrich and bless my life. Your support and input is such a treasured gift.

And to all of you who are reading this book and have the courage to keep growing and learning despite your circumstances!

A very special thank you to:

Lynn Wagner – I can't imagine not having you there to capture all this through your creative digital eye! Thank you for all your support and artistic input. I treasure your sisterhood and the bond we have!

Georgeann Gobel – My wonderful assistant (in my workshops) and one of my best friends in the whole wide world. Your incredible support and encouragement have made a huge difference in my life. Thank you for being a true servant of God.

Robin Cooley – Thank you for being there to encourage me to check out raw and stick with me through all kinds of growing times. Thanks for doing the dishes in the early days of workshops! You are another wonder in this world!

Elaine Wright Colvin – Your wisdom and guidance helped me take some huge steps forward!

To the following people who have supported me in the creation, implementation, and impartation of both this book and my workshops, thank you:

Tina Cochran and Cheri Van Elgort for doing dishes and assisting me in the early classes. Donna Stoddard for coming on board with your raw knowledge, experience and wonderful assistant skills. Your support and encouragement are invaluable! Dan Wagner for your patient technical support. Sandy Corlett, I so appreciate you encouraging me and directing me in the early days of writing the book. Janet Thompson, thank you so much for all your great questions, feedback and support. Rod Heskett for listening and giving me such helpful feedback and business support. Jeff Eldred your wise counsel, encouragement and support have been monumental. Dan Kline, Kay Strom and Jon Vonhoff, you are all awesome mentors and I am so grateful!

All those at Trader Joe's and Organic By Nature who make each of these such great companies to do business with (you know who you are—Sondi Bergmann and Jason Hammond, Scott Ertz, Cindy Stuehler, Walter Longria, David Sandoval, Michael Wohlfeldl and crew). Thank you all for your very cherished support. Thank you also to Catherine Barr for being such a great Market Manager for our local farmers' market and for the opportunity to share *RawSome Recipes* with our market community.

A huge thank you and much applause to Su Gatch and Marianne Wyllie for transforming the layout, editing and design of the book with your masterful graphic artistry. Bravo! Lastly, and with much gratitude, thanks to Brian Manwaring, Paul Springer and Essential Science Publishing for making the publishing of this book possible.

Foreword

By Janet Thompson

*M*eeting Robyn Boyd at the Mt. Hermon Writer's Conference and getting to know her and her passion for nutritious eating has changed my life and quite possibly saved it. I am a breast cancer survivor and part of my healing therapy has been eating more raw, organic, sugar-free and preservative-free foods. Our bodies are a temple created by God and how we take care of that temple reflects the value we place on this gift.

When I first met Robyn at the conference and she heard I was recovering from cancer she said something that convinced me, "We are not eating the way God planned for us to eat." That struck my heart and I knew she was right. I had fallen into the trap of quick meals and using processed foods and had frankly gotten bored with cooking. I had strayed far from God's original plan for how I was to eat. I was a dietitian for 17 years and so at first I thought I would know more than Robyn, but I soon found out I was wrong.

I have made some radical changes in the eating habits of my family, and others are noticing how healthy and thin my husband and I look. Our transition has not been a fad diet that eliminates whole food groups. Instead, we are still eating the four basic food groups, but preparing them in a way that maintains their original nutrition and just eliminating those foods that are harmful to our body. If you are wondering how to do that, Robyn and her book *RawSome Recipes* have been my mentor and resource through this dietary journey. It has been fun and educational, learning and applying principles that help rather than hinder health. You will find you need far less medications and doctor's visits if you are putting into your body the fuel that it needs to run efficiently and safely.

I recently had a test we all dread. I will give you a clue; it was performed by a gastroenterologist. It is the dreaded colonoscopy... a test, I might add, that has saved millions of lives. When I had this same test five years ago, several polyps were detected and I was told to come back in three years. This time, I heard the best words I could ever hear from the doctor, "You have a very healthy colon. We will see you in five years." One of my friends who knows about my dietary changes summed it all up when she heard this report and said, "It has to be all the healthy eating you have been doing!" I fully agree.

Another thing I have noticed is that God made food so beautiful in its natural state. When you serve wholesome foods that have not been treated with chemicals and are as close to their raw state as possible, you will be amazed at your effortless, beautiful and colorful food presentations. If at all possible I highly recommend taking one of Robyn's RawSome workshops and learning how to apply the many wonderful tips and recipes she provides. Also take her suggestion to slowly change over your eating habits. You might feel overwhelmed if you try everything at once but as you use up things in your pantry, replace them with more nutritious products. Even if you have already been eating healthy, you will probably learn new ideas and techniques from Robyn. Her workshops are fun, interactive and full of energy. I want everyone I know to be able to experience one for themselves. She really makes her book come alive!

Janet Thompson is an author and national speaker. She is the founder and director of Woman To Woman Mentoring, *and author of* "Woman to Woman Mentoring: How To Start, Grow, and Maintain A Mentoring Ministry" *and* "Dear God, They Say It's Cancer." *Janet has a Bachelor of Science degree in Food Administration from California Polytechnic University, an MBA from California Lutheran University, and an MA in Christian Leadership from Fuller Theological Seminary.*

Preface

The reason I call my recipes **RAWSOME** is because you will find that they are mostly **RAW** with **SOME** organic whole cooked foods. 75% of the recipes in this book use all raw foods. Ninety-three percent of the recipes are all vegan.

For optimum health I recommend eating simply, purely, wholly, and 75–80% raw!

Whether you are pure raw vegan, lacto-vegetarian, or just transitioning to healthier eating, you will find recipes to please your palate.

Making food to please your family and encourage children to eat well and enjoy the process of making meals is also a goal of this book. You will find many recipes my daughter loves and has voted as "kid friendly." The recipes that have gone over well with my daughter Molly and her friends, (approx. ages 4–14) have been labeled: **"RawSome Kid Recipe!"** You may want to try these recipes first, keeping in mind that every child has different tastes that they are drawn to. This is just a guideline from my child to yours. We would love to hear what works with your family and any recipes that you create! It really is fun to get the whole family involved. It is a great way to grow and hang out together. Everyone can relate to food. So get Grandma and Grandpa in there with you too! Have fun and enjoy the recipes!

At the end of the recipes you will find *Planning Meals Ahead* to help you get organized. *Fit for Company... Four All-Raw Dinner Menus* will help you take the stress out of what to make for guests! For those festive occasions, you will find a *RawSome Holiday Menu*. *Great After School Snacks and Grazing Foods* will give you fabulous healthy ideas to please the kids. Get super ideas for snacks while other kids are over on play dates. *Tips for Healthy Traveling* is an important and helpful section to help you stay healthy and happy while traveling, minimizing being at the mercy of all those toxins and pollutants out there! *Essential Oils for Home and Travel* will help you get further down the road on a healthier footing.

Eat well and be well!

Cheers,

Robyn Boyd

wrboyd@earthlink.net

Table of Contents

Table of Contents, cont.

RawSome Information 1

Discernment in a World of Choices

"What is the perfect diet for me?" you might ask. "But I thought eating soy was good for me and what about that canola oil? Are protein powders really not good? What about the drawer full of expensive vitamins and supplements? Which foods really are providing 'superior' nutrition? How come they tell me to drink distilled water and now I'm hearing that is bad too? All my favorite foods—they tell me they are no good and now I can't even drink the water!!! Help! But whom can I trust to be the ultimate source of truth? This person says the Bible clearly states we are to eat only fruits, veggies, nuts and seeds. That person claims the Bible says we can eat anything." Do you have any thoughts like these?

There are many theories, beliefs, and convictions about diet and health. If you have ever even dabbled a little bit into the vast array of information out there about nutrition you will agree that it is a can of worms. So who do you follow? What do you believe?

How can any one diet be for all people? We are all unique creations. Different bodies require different things. If you are a sprouting teen your body requirements are quite different from a woman plunging into menopause. If you commute two hours a day amidst rows of fossil fuel-burning hunks of metal and catch a jelly-oozing donut on the way to your job as an air traffic controller, your body will require many things, especially over time. In contrast, if all that is required of you for work each day is that you ever so preciously water the bonsai collection of a certain notorious millionaire who happens to be your spouse; a smoothie on the pool deck after a game of tennis may be all you need! Add to the mix that we all have differing metabolisms and you find that consumption content and amounts can vary greatly.

...don't make food your religion.

Make it your wisdom!

Who is in the position to clearly judge what you should or should not do, or what you do or don't require? Am I to be your "food police?" Oh heavens no! Are you to become so rigid that you turn into your own "food police" and that of your family? God forbid! No, the point here isn't to take away all your fun and impose all kinds of rules and laws that must be enforced under no uncertain terms. Furthermore, don't make food your religion. Make it your wisdom!

There are however, some conclusions about food and diet that can be related to the whole of humanity. It seems as though we live in a time of what I call the silent Third World War. What do I mean by this bold statement? The use of pesticides, germicides, fluoride, chlorine, petroleum and God only knows the list of man-made chemicals that have seeped into our air, land and sea are now out of control. The effect all this poisoning is having on our bodies is incomparable to any other time in history.

Remember the old Bible scripture often quoted: *"For the love of money is a root of all kinds of evil."* (*1 Timothy 6:9-11 NIV*).

There is huge money to be made not only in the pharmaceutical industry but also the "natural" foods and supplement industry as well. Everywhere you look there is another product to be sold to cure what ails you. The marketplace is full of schemes, hypes, multi-level networks, gimmicks and gizmos. We are constantly being bombarded with brilliant advertising that convinces us of our need to consume. All this consumption costs us. It costs us environmentally, socially, politically and, saddest of all, spiritually. We look to the world to fix us, save us, rescue us and fulfill us. We bypass the goodness God has provided. We look for the packaged natural remedy or food and forsake God's simple gifts from the garden.

We eat at restaurants whose sauces and salad dressings are laden with MSG hidden in deceptive ways. When we go out to restaurants, which are commonplace in our fast-paced world, we eat food dripping in rancid oils, over-salted and zapped in microwaves. In our frantic pace we look for ways to make life more convenient so we eat denatured fast and frozen foods. With our constant cultural conditioning to look thin, we attempt all kinds of diets and consume chemicals that we think will cut the corners and cut the fat from our fluffy, bloated, overladen and toxic bodies.

We ingest excitotoxins* and have no clue what those are and what they really do. We get these excitotoxins in various forms through artificial sweeteners and MSG. These artificial sweeteners are wed with artificial stimulants and made into diet drinks. Everywhere you look in public places there are advertisements encouraging everyone, at any age, to ingest these toxic drinks. Look around at all the soda drinking invitations. They are there to greet you at every gas station, movie theatre, restaurant, airport, airplane, sports event and on and on. We talk on radioactive phones. We drink bottled water that commingles in plastic bottles until it hits your lips. Our city drinking water is contaminated as well as our lakes, streams and oceans. We eat garbage food while we watch garbage television! Our meat, fish and poultry have been exposed to such incredible amounts of poisoning and disease-creating circumstances. What was once fit in Biblical times no longer remains true today!

It is staggering when you think about the amount of chemicals that bombard and assault us daily. The other day I went to lick an envelope closed to send off a bill to a local department store. The whole thing reeked of perfume and as I licked the flap closed I got perfume on my tongue! Doesn't that just make your taste buds shiver? Did you ever think about what it takes to make perfume or what that actually does to the body? If you care to know more about the effects of chemical perfumes try exploring the following site:

http://www.ameliaww.com/fpin/Commentary2.html

Excitotoxin: "A substance added to foods and beverages that literally stimulates neurons to death, causing brain damage of varying degrees. Can be found in such ingredients as monosodium glutamate, aspartame (NutraSweet), cystein, hydrolyzed protein, and aspartic acid." From the back cover of *Excitotoxins: The Taste That Kills* by Russell Blaylock, MD.

Steps We Can Take Toward Living Wholly

There are so many wonderful books available now that go into technical details about all of the concerns I have just mentioned. See the recommended reading list at the back of the book if you would like to further educate yourself. Rather than belabor how bad it all is, I would prefer to focus on the foods God has given us and what we have the power to do through proper education, wise choices and implementation.

- **Gradually eliminate all products from your life and home that have chemicals.** Each week work on eliminating one more toxic item from your life like sugar or caffeine. Replace each unhealthy choice with trying one new thing like drinking plenty of water daily or making almond milk to replace cow's milk. Go slow and keep refining! Letting go of the old takes time but the benefits of the new are so worth it. Give your new lifestyle choices time and soon you will see great benefits. The more raw food you add, the more health and energy you will experience.

- **As much as possible consume organic food.**

- **If you consume animal products, make sure you buy quality free-range and organically fed with no hormones or antibiotics given.** Animal products should be used sparingly if at all. Absolutely stay away from all pork.

- **If choosing to eat fish it is best to select deep-sea fish coming from clean water, not farmed.** Don't be fooled by labeling saying fish is "fresh" or "Atlantic." These words may lead you to think the fish was not farmed.

- **Exercise regularly.**

- **When possible, expose yourself to 20 minutes of sun a day.**

- **Get adequate rest.**

- **Eat whole foods coming in the form God made them, not invented or processed by man.**

- **Try to eat mostly raw fruits and vegetables so as to increase enzymes.**

- **Practice good eating habits including good food combining.** Chew foods slowly and well.

- **Drink plenty of good clean filtered water.** Some suggest half your body weight in ounces per day.

- **When eating oil, make sure all sources are organic, including butter** (as chemicals bond to fats). The best oils are olive and coconut.

- **Avoid the many hazards of microwaved cooking.**

- **Take time to listen and get quiet...** Many find daily prayer and quiet time to be extremely helpful. Both prayer and laughter are incredible healing agents.

Whole Foods the Way God Intended

What exactly makes up a whole food diet? A wide variety of multi-colored fruits, veggies, nuts, seeds and legumes are examples of foods made by God to nourish and sustain our bodies. What we are looking for is foods in their whole food form. Why eat whole organic foods? Because that is the way they come to us in nature and because the sum of an object is greater than its lesser parts. The elements that make up a piece of fruit for example, work together synergistically. A good example of this is an orange, having the bioflavinoids contained in the membranous whitish skin. If we denature food, then we leave out elements that create a complete or whole nutritional package that God intended as nourishment for our bodies.

When we take milk and pasteurize it or homogenize it, we now have a different food. The nutrient value changes dramatically and ends up costing our body to be able to assimilate and digest it in this altered form. Some people term foods that have been altered or used in part as fractured foods.

The recipes I have included in this book use whole foods. Optimally, it is best to get these foods organic and as freshly picked as is possible. Of whole foods, the absolute best are those foods that are still living. Living foods mean they are still alive and growing. Once you pick an apple off the tree it is no longer connected to the source that courses through it to make it continue to grow. It will not get any larger once off the branch. Sunflower sprouts, in contrast, are a living food. They are still thriving when you pop them in your mouth, as long as they haven't sat around too long.

Seventy-five percent of the recipes in this book use all raw foods. Ninety-three percent of the recipes are all vegan. For people who are transitioning to healthier eating or those who include small amounts of quality animal protein there are just a handful of recipes that include hard boiled eggs and organic raw goat cheese and goat yogurt.

Here is an interesting scripture that endorses the use of goats' milk: *"The lambs are for thy clothing, and the goats are the price of the field. And thou shalt have goats' milk enough for thy food, for the food of thy household, and for the maintenance for thy maidens."* (Proverbs 27:27 KJV)

Shifting to Whole Foods

Replace the old with the new. Renew your mind by thinking of this change not as having to give things up but instead the chance to find new and better things.

Replace the Old	Embrace the New
Sugar	Agave, honey or dates
Coffee	Caffeine-free herbal teas
White rice	Brown rice, whole grains
White bread, refined flours	Whole wheat and multi-grain bread
Cow's milk	Goat, almond, rice and oat milk
Regular eggs	Brown fertile eggs with no hormones
Canned foods	Fresh fruits and veggies
Frozen, packaged, foods	Fresh whole foods
Processed oils	Organic olive oil, coconut oil, Udo's Choice Oil
All mayonnaise	Vegenaise
Ketchups with sugar	Fruit juice sweetened ketchup
Cheese	Raw rennetless goat cheese
Table salt	Celtic Sea Salt or Real Salt

Embracing the New

If you have made it this far in the book, going a page at a time, I will assume that you are wanting to, willing and able to, or have made some sort of change in your diet. For some it is a question of tightening up the loose edges. For others this is radical. Wherever you are, feel encouraged. Change is possible!

Each time you go shopping, replace old items with new and healthier versions. Think of it as upgrading. You will notice that buying "health food" and all organic can be much more costly. If you have a Trader Joe's market in your area shop there first. You will find that they stock a wonderful range of organic items at very decent prices. It is always a pleasure to go there and find such wonderful savings on so many foods that I use as staples. You will see that your organic dollars will stretch way further there. Even though eating all organic is more expensive, just think of all the money you are going to save by not having to pay medical expenses! The time that this way of eating will also cost you is going to save you much precious time wasted sitting in doctor's offices! It is all so worth it!

One of the first items I recommend that you buy would be Mason jars with screw tight lids. Thrift stores, garage sales and flea markets are all great places to buy jars cheap. Storing your staples in glass jars is a wonderful way to prolong the shelf life of your food. I use the largest size for items like nuts, grains, and legumes. Spices can be stored in small glass jars.

You can begin by buying any or all of the following staples. Replace all your old canned foods with a variety of brightly colored whole foods and store them in air tight Mason jars:

Dried fruits:
dried apricots
shredded coconut
currants
dried papaya
dried persimmons
raisins
sun dried tomatoes

Fresh staples:
(*can be stored/displayed in baskets*
on countertops)
apples
avocados
bananas
garlic
ginger
lemons
limes
tomatoes

Grains:
barley
brown rice
couscous
millet
oats
quinoa
bulgar wheat
corn meal
whole wheat flour

Legumes:
black beans
garbanzo beans
kidney beans
dried green peas
lentils
pinto beans

Nuts and seeds:
almonds
cashews
flaxseeds
macadamia nuts
pecans
pumpkin seeds
sesame seeds
sunflower seeds
walnuts

Spices and oils:
carob powder
cinnamon
Celtic Sea Salt or Real Salt
cumin powder
curry powder
dill
garlic powder
ginger powder
onion flakes
onion powder
psyllium powder
pumpkin spice
red pepper flakes
turmeric
raw vanilla bean
organic coconut oil
organic olive oil
Udo's Oil

Other staples:
agave
cook's vanilla
raw almond butter
unsweetened apricot jam
honey
Nama shoyu
raw tahini
Vegenaise

Thrifty and Nifty Kitchen Gear

If money is limited, one of the best investments for this way of cooking would be a food processor. The best I have found at a decent price is made by Hamilton Beach. I found mine at Target for $29. Used or barely used food processors and blenders are also commonly found at garage sales as leftovers from wedding gifts! Look around, there are tons out there waiting for you at a great price.

Aside from the obvious, like an assortment of sharp kitchen knives, mixing bowl and cooking and serving utensils, I have compiled a beginner's list of items that should carry you through the preparations of the recipes in this book.

Blender

Kitchen scissors

Strainers (2 or 3)

Glass Mason jars

Lemon juice squeezer

Peeler

Measuring cups

Measuring spoons

Stainless steel bowls in assorted sizes

Scraping spatula

Chopper (I love the chopper made by Pampered Chef)

Food processor – Target (approx. $29 made by Hamilton Beach) or if money is no object the best processor is Cuisinart (best price at Costco)

Nut milk bag (see Almond Milk recipe for where to get this)

Spiral slicer (see pesto and marinara recipe page for how to order)

Assorted round glass storage containers with plastic lids – (Cost Plus)

Coffee grinder (great for grinding up flaxseeds and making *Gamazio*)

Several stainless steel mesh colander baskets in assorted sizes – (try Cost Plus)

Juicers, dehydrators, blenders – I recommend the Visor, The Norwalk Press, and the Champion Juicer (see *Helpful Websites*). For the money the Visor is the best. This state of the art juicer does everything including wheatgrass, all fruits and veggies plus makes pastas and ice creams! I sell them at the lowest possible prices. Call me for more information on juicers, dehydrators and blenders.

Whole Food Supplements

For the most part, I like to eat all my foods as close to whole and organic as possible. However, there are a few supplements that I use and find extreme benefit from. I consider these my whole food supplement staples.

Barley grass

Barley grass is a wonderful way for vegetarians to get all essential amino acids. Amino acids are the building blocks of proteins, which are the major components of every cell in the body. Barley grass contains polypeptides, which are smaller proteins, making them more easily absorbed directly into the bloodstream where they promote cell metabolism. Loaded with valuable enzymes and a wide spectrum of vitamins and minerals, barley grass powder becomes a whole food concentrate.

The chlorophyll in this grass is as close to human hemoglobin as is found in nature. Chlorophyll's benefits are numerous but one that is quite impressive according to an article in the *Journal of the National Cancer Institute* (Jan. 4, 1995) states that chlorophyll fed to laboratory animals was found to reduce absorption of three dietary carcinogens. This is an excellent way to help maintain a healthy acid-alkaline balance essential in preventing many diseases. Barley grass coupled with raw vegetable juicing (especially carrot) is one of the best super foods I've seen to benefit patients recovering from cancer. There are several highly beneficial brands of barley on the market today. I prefer Just Barley by Pure Planet or Pure Barley by Platinum Health Products* over other brands because they don't use maltodextrin (it is just pure barley, nothing else). This is especially good news for people with blood sugar issues! Some say the maltodextrin used in other products is not a problem. Barley Life by the Aim Corporation and Barley Max from Hallelujah Acres are also popular barley products. It is best to try what works well in your own body.

Bee pollen

I love adding bee pollen into smoothies or just eating it straight off a heaping teaspoon in the morning. This is a wonderful way to get your B-complex vitamins, which are essential especially during stressful times. It is an immune strengthener loaded with vitamins, amino acids, essential fatty acids and minerals and is comprised of approximately 15 percent protein. Some people are allergic to it so it is best to start out with a very small amount like ⅛ of a teaspoon and work up slowly to about 1 teaspoon, watching for any reactions.

Brewer's yeast

My favorite brewer's yeast is made by Twinlab and called SuperRich Yeast Plus. It contains GTF chromium and selenium which is wonderful for helping to maintain blood sugar levels. Most people who know about brewer's yeast think about it in terms of being a good source of B vitamins. However, yeast's value goes on to include 16 amino acids and approximately 15 minerals. By weight it is 52% protein. Known to be helpful for eczema, heart disorders, anxiety and fatigue, brewer's yeast is a great immune enhancer and seems to increase energy and mental clarity.

Chlorella

According to Platinum Health Products:* "Chlorella is nature's richest whole food source of chlorophyll (providing 1.7 to 3 percent), a powerful cleanser and detoxifier. Studies have indicated

*You can find out more or make an order at **www.platinumhealthproducts.com/rawsome**, or call 888-747-6733. Use referral code 1114 when ordering to receive a 20% discount.

that chlorella may help lower cholesterol because of it high Omega-3 essential fatty acid content. In Japan, where chlorella is the #1 supplement, it is commonly recommended to aid the body in the elimination of heavy metals and other toxins such as DDT, mercury, cadmium and lead.

Essential fatty acids—the good, the bad and the ugly!

Let's start with the ugly fats—hydrogenated fats like margarine and shortening are the worst and can cause heart disease. Chemically fried fats are known as junk fats and can be seen on package labels as "partially hydrogenated" or "hydrogenated" and are found in most cookies and crackers. These oils have been fried with hydrogen and metal for prolonged periods of time. The purpose of this is to change them from their natural liquid state into solid trans-fats. These type of fats will absolutely lead to heart disease as the body cannot process it properly. The inevitable build up on the arterial walls seriously impairs the blood flow.

Butter is a saturated fat that can actually help lower tryglycerides. Did you know that butter is the best and most easily absorbed source of Vitamin A? It also contains the antioxidants selenium and vitamin E. You just can't beat the quality of the vitamin A that butter provides, which is essential for promoting healthy growth in children. One drawback is that eaten too often, butter can inhibit the benefits of the essential omega 3 and 6 fats. If you choose to eat butter, do so in moderation and only use organic.

Essential fats are *essential*, hence we need quality fat on a regular basis:

- for the production of all hormones
- to protect our internal organs
- to burn for fuel when food is not readily available
- to help maintain our sex drive
- to maintain mental clarity
- to avoid carbohydrate cravings
- to keep our bowels working properly
- to help some women avoid fertility problems
- to act as barriers in our cells to keep out harmful microbes
- to maintain healthy hair, skin and to combat eczema
- to help support neuron connections vital in the brain's communication system
- because nerve, brain, eye, heart, adrenal and thyroid cells require essential fats to function
- because fat is necessary for the production of serotonin, which is key in elevating mood and promoting sleep.
- to maintain healthy heart and arteries
- to treat diabetic neuropathy
- to relieve PMS and cyclical breast pain
- to prevent gallstones
- because it will actually help with weight loss (Omega 3 fats raise our metabolic rate and act as diuretics, helping kidneys flush excess water from tissues)

The best oils to use are:

Olive oil, coconut oil, Pacific Hemp Supreme 7 Oil Blend, Udo's Choice Oil Blend and grapeseed, as in Vegenaise mayonnaise, are all good oils to use. Grapeseed, olive and coconut oils can all withstand very high temperatures so they are good for cooking. See benefits of coconut oil below, and in *Glossary of Ingredients* in the *RawSome Resources* section.

Tip: Try using coconut oil instead of butter. Also add coconut oil or Udo's Oil to fruit smoothies to slow down the intake of the sugar. This will make it easier on the pancreas to process and will help keep blood sugar levels a little more even.

Coconut oil

Coconut oil is being crowned as one of the world's most beneficial whole foods and oils. Research has proven that the fat content of coconuts is made up primarily of medium-chain triglycerides, which are used immediately in the body as an energy source. They do not circulate in the blood stream as fat, leading to weight gain and other health problems. Many health benefits from the use of this heart-healthy oil are now being discovered. Studies indicate effectiveness against parasites, fungus and viruses. Great benefits, such as preventing osteoporosis, improving digestion and nutrient absorption are heralded. Coconut oil is marvelous for keeping the skin soft and smooth, and may help prevent premature aging and wrinkles. For 100% pure extra-virgin organic coconut oil I recommend Tropic Oil, which is distributed by Platinum Health Products (see footnote, pg. 16).

Flaxseeds

Another marvelous way to obtain the omega 3 fatty acids is to grind up 1/4 cup of flaxseeds in a small coffee grinder and add to smoothies. Also a good source of protein, B vitamins and zinc. Good for reducing the pain and inflammation of arthritis, found to lower cholesterol and triglyceride levels as well as maintaining bowels.

Garlic

Volumes have been written about garlic. One of garlic's greatest values is its natural antibiotic effect. Did you know it was used to prevent gangrene during World War I? Also very effective with fungal infections like candida, common athlete's foot and vaginitis. Research is being done using garlic to destroy certain viruses like herpes, fever blisters and smallpox, as well as colds and flu. Another great way to build up the immune system!

Hylands' Herbal Calms Forte

Although this is not a "whole food" I just had to throw it into the mix. Made from all natural herbs, I've used this for years on those nights when I just can't sleep. Whether you are wired, menopausal, or anxious this herbal homeopathic remedy does the job like no other I've tried with absolutely no side affects the next morning! Thank God for Herbal Calms!

Kelp granules

Kelp is a type of seaweed rich in B vitamins as well as many minerals. Kelp is often used to help treat thyroid problems because of the iodine content. Known to protect against the effects of radiation, it is good to use for cancer patients and those receiving X-rays. Also said to be helpful for brain tissue. Kelp can be purchased as granules and used as a condiment on soups, salads and baked potatoes. We use it instead of pepper.

Probiotics

It is essential to take probiotics when one takes any kind of antibiotic to help maintain the "friendly bacteria" in the digestive tract. Just taking yogurt or kefir isn't strong enough. Probiotics help to promote the proper digestion of food, and is a great aid when undigested food causes the body to produce histamine, resulting in allergic symptoms. Probiotics are great for all kinds of stomach upsets, and especially good to take when stomach flu is going around or at the first hints of food poisoning.

One problem with most probiotics is their short shelf life, and the need to refrigerate them. Platinum Health Products (see web address and phone number on pg. 16) offers an amazing new combination of vital bacteria in a shelf-stable form that maintains its potency without refrigeration. They have combined strains of scientifically validated beneficial bacteria including prebiotics called fructo-oligosaccharides with acacia gum that "feeds" the growth of the "friendly trio" L-sporogenes. To this, they have added F-19, a newly-discovered probiotic that is thought to stimulate wellness in the digestive tract. My hunch is there are several other companies making as good or superior products.

Daily Fiber Blend

This product is one of the gentlest I've tried for cleansing and restoring the colon. This is an essential way to eliminate old toxic waste and establish optimum health. It is made from all natural, mostly organic, plant based ingredients and ground into a fine powder that when mixed with juice or water is taken once or twice a day. The specific fibers used enhance bowel function; gently cleansing and eliminating accumulated waste as well as LDL or "bad" cholesterol in our blood and tissues. It also contains 18 proteins including all nine essential amino acids in a balanced and highly digestible form. This is one of the purest formulas I have found for this type of application. You won't believe how good you will feel! (I have found that it is essential when taking this to drink an abundance of water.) **Detoxification is a key to health and weight loss**. Distributed by Platinum Health Products (seeweb address and phone on pg. 16).

Ingredients list: Nova Scotia Pumpkin Seed Meal, Organic Ground Flax, Rice Bran, Rice Protein, Psyllium Husk, Natural Apple Fibers, Soya Lecithin, Organic Jerusalem Artichoke, Organic Ground Chia, Organic Fennel Seed, Organic Sprouted Quinoa, Organic Sprouted Amaranth, Organic Sprouted Spelt, Organic Sprouted Kamut, Pineapple, Konjac Root, Walnut.

Shiitake mushrooms

A great super food, containing eighteen amino acids, B vitamins, and a polysaccharide known as lentinan, which increases T cell function strengthening the immune system. Shiitakes are also known to be very effective in treating cancer.

Spirulina

According to the folks at Organic By Nature, who make my favorite spirulina, "This is nature's richest source of protein, containing more than three times the protein in fish, poultry or red meat. Spirulina is also very high in calcium (containing five times more calcium than whole milk), beta-carotene and essential fatty acids. Many people use spirulina as antioxidant protection, a weight loss aid, protein powder, energy supplement and immune system enhancer. Spirulina is a whole food, so you can safely eat as much or little as you like with or without meals."

I could not be happier with the Carob Mint Spirulina made by Organic By Nature. This daily food has brought some of the best results that I have ever personally experienced, as well as in others. Pure

Hawaiian premium-grade spirulina without carob mint flavor is also available through Platinum Health Products.

Wheatgrass

A potent detoxifier rich with chlorophyll and a wide variety of vitamins and minerals much like barley grass. I suggest starting out slowly. When fresh is not available, I recommend Green Kamut Wheatgrass from Organic By Nature. This is what they say about it: "Wheatgrass has been served 'fresh' at juice bars for over 30 years as one of nature's most rejuvenating foods. Our 100% pure, certified organic Green Kamut powder contains the power of wheatgrass juice (65%) combined with alfalfa leaf juice (35%). This non-pasteurized concentrate is guaranteed to be mild tasting and as effective as 'fresh' (or your money back). Our ancient Egyptian wheatgrass (Kamut), and alfalfa juice powders are grown high in the mountains in Utah, watered with only spring water and dried at a low temperature (below 88° F) to create the most potent wheatgrass juice powder on the market."

For the ultimate grass blend, including the finest wheatgrass, grown from the ancient Egyptian kamut seed, I recommend Organic Kamut Blend made by Platinum Health Products (see web address and phone on pg. 16). The kamut is complimented by the sweet taste of oatgrass juice and mineral-rich juice from mature alfalfa leaves.

Note: I am learning all the time about new products and supplements, so please do your own research. It is a constant refining process for me to find better and purer products. What may work in my body may not work in yours. I just share this list as information and possible confirmation!

What About Vitamin B12?

A common argument against vegetarianism is that one will become deficient in vitamin B12. What people fail to realize is that both vegetarians and meat eaters can come up short in this department. The only way B12 is manufactured is by bacteria and specific algae. The reason animal products and plants contain B12 has to do with the fact that bacteria will grow in these foods. When there is an adequate amount of the trace element cobalt, then bacteria growing in foods such as eggs, milk, and flesh foods will leave B12 as a contributing residue.

Although washing our hands, food and cooking utensils is an important practice, we inadvertently dramatically decrease the amount of the necessary B12 residue that our bodies require and should be receiving from the bacteria found on our foods.

When we aren't receiving the proper supply of B12 what can result is nerve degeneration and other important cell damage. Symptoms that might arise as a result of deficiency are a loss of feeling in fingers and toes or in the spine. Other symptoms may include loss of balance with clumsiness, decreased reflex responses, increased irritability, memory loss, lack of concentration and depression.

The best way to give your body B12 is by taking brewer's yeast, bee pollen, sea vegetables or algae. Equally important is the need to withhold ingesting alcohol, tobacco, coffee, birth control pills and antibiotics as these substances create an increased need of B12.

When we cook our food we destroy anywhere from 30–90% of the B12, says Gabriel Cousens, M.D. in his book *Conscious Eating*. He has a very informative chapter (called "Do Vegetarians Get Enough Vitamin B12?"), if you want to go into more depth on this subject.

The Value of Sea Vegetables

Good sea vegetables to consider adding to your diet are: kelp, alaria, arame, kombu, hijiki, wakambe, dulse and nori. Spirulina is an excellent choice as well.

For thousands of years people all around the world have been eating and enjoying the health benefits derived from sea vegetables. The recent success of sushi bars that have sprung up across America has helped to introduce more people to sea vegetables. We have begun to associate the use of seaweeds, like those used to make sushi, as a trademark of the Japanese culture. However, people from such varied cultures as the Australian Aborigines, the Native American Indians and the Atlantic coastal people of the British Isles, France and Scandinavia have also been eating these oceanic veggies for hundreds of years as well.

Aside from being a great source of protein and calcium, the minerals in sea vegetation are found in very similar ratios as those found in blood. This food is a great complex carbohydrate with carotenes and chlorophyll to add to the list of reasons to consider learning to incorporate this food into your diet.

If you haven't tried sea veggies before, then starting with vegetarian sushi is your best bet. The California roll with mac nuts substituted for the crabmeat is a favorite with my family. Ever since my daughter Molly was little, her body must have craved the nutrients in nori (which is the outer seaweed wrapping used to make sushi) because she used to eat sheets and sheets of nori. She still requests it often as a snack. She began eating seaweeds very early on and absolutely loves sushi. Another favorite for her is seaweed salad, which can often be found at sushi bars and Japanese restaurants. Some of the health food stores, especially ones that have delis, like Whole Foods, also sell seaweed salad. At our favorite sushi bar we have found that they use fresh seaweed, which has a much different taste than seaweeds that have been dried and then rehydrated. Fresh seaweed salad is a delicious delicacy! Unfortunately, seaweed salad from restaurants often contains sugar.

Another easy way to introduce sea veggies into your life is to take a strip of kombu and cut it into half-inch pieces with kitchen scissors. Include kombu pieces when making soups, stews, or in your cooking water when making beans or rice. Hijiki is another type of seaweed I use. It is good to soak hijiki in filtered water for at least 30 minutes and then drain. Each piece swells up and becomes what we call a seaweed noodle! Hijiki can be stirred into a pot of fresh cooked brown rice or made into a special salad.

Quick Tip on Soaking and Sprouting

It is important to soak nuts and seeds to wash off naturally occurring growth inhibitors. This is to prevent them from sprouting prematurely, should drops of water penetrate the skins. Soaking and sprouting helps to pre-digest food, as the fats are broken down into fatty acids and the proteins into amino acids. The recipes that require soaking will specify how long to soak. It is best to soak almonds up to 24 hours (rinsing twice a day) as the fat content can be reduced significantly. Most small legumes like lentil, mung and adzuki only require two to three hours of soaking. When you soak them longer they get waterlogged and do not sprout very well.

Getting Enough Calcium and Protein

Some people have been so indoctrinated to believe that milk is the only way to get adequate supplies of calcium that they lapse into a state of regression when they attempt to change their diet. But rest assured that there are many foods that supply the nutritional components found in dairy milk. You will find that almonds, beans, peas, spirulina, whole grains and greens such as kale supply ample amounts of calcium. There have been many studies done proving that without the heavy intake of animal protein that actually robs the body of calcium to be able to digest these foods, we don't require as much calcium as what was once believed.

In terms of protein, the time the body requires the most amount of protein due to the rapid growth period is in infancy. It takes a human baby 180 days to double the birth weight. However, did you know that 1 cup of human breast milk only contains 2.4 gm of protein and 80 mg of calcium? Think about that! The human baby with blossoming growth, rapid weight gain and developing organs only requires 2.4 grams of protein per cup! Only 5% of the calories come from protein. (By the way, almond milk contains only 2 grams of protein per cup, coming in very close to human milk protein content.)

Cows, on the other hand, produce milk with 8.5 gm of protein and 288 mg of calcium. That is a big difference—roughly four times the amount of protein and more than three times the amount of calcium. A baby calf doubles its birth weight in only 47 days, which is approximately four times as fast as us humans. Because of this rapid development the protein in milk for baby calves contains 15% protein, as compared to 5% for baby humans. Guess where the mama cow gets the protein to produce the protein found in her milk. You guessed it, from eating green grass! That's right. That big old heifer cow gets all the protein she requires to make all that meat and bones from grass! So where on earth did we get the notion that human beings needed to wean off of mother's milk onto an ongoing diet including the milk from the mother of a baby calf?! Just what is the wisdom of that?

Just a few more "raw" facts on milk and animal protein:

- ⚘ Animal fats, including dairy and eggs, are saturated fats and have been found to be a factor in heart and artery disease. The only place we find cholesterol is in animal products.

- ⚘ The most common food sensitivity in this country comes from dairy product consumption. Symptoms include chronic ear, nose and throat infections as well as bronchial infections and other inflammations.

- ⚘ Diseases in children like Type I diabetes and leukemia have been linked to dairy consumption.

- ⚘ Breast cancer risks increase with a high intake of animal protein.

- ⚘ Countries with the highest incidence of osteoporosis also have the highest intake of dairy products.

- ⚘ The body is required to use up calcium in order to process the excessive protein and phosphate content of dairy products.

Food	Quantity	Protein	Calcium
Almonds	¼ cup	6.6 gm	82 mg
Barley grass*	3 T.	9.0 gm	61 mg
Blackstrap molasses	1 T.	0.0 gm	137 mg
Broccoli	1 cup	4.8 gm	135 mg
Butternut squash	1 cup	3.7 gm	82 mg
Collards	1 cup	5.4 gm	300 mg
Dried figs	5	2.9 gm	135 mg
Kale (cooked)	1 cup	6.4 gm	270 mg
Kamut, wheatgrass*	3 T.	4.5 gm	50 mg
Orange	1 large	2.3 gm	76 mg
Navy beans	1 cup	14.8 gm	94 mg
Spirulina*	3 T.	6.0 gm	80 mg
Sunflower seeds	2 T.	4.3 gm	21 mg
Tahini	1 T.	2.6 gm	64 mg

Source: Cross-referenced from various research and the Wimar Institute's New Start Lifestyle Cookbook
*Sourced from Organic By Nature

The Negatives of Eating Soy

For a long time we have heard the praises sung about soy products, especially tofu and tempeh. Just when you thought you had found a great meat alternative and wonderful protein source, the news flashes and the tide turns against soy! The best site I have found to simply summarize the issues with soy can be found at **www.westonaprice.org/soy_ alert.htm**. Check it out and find out what works best in your unique body!

Balancing Acid and Alkaline Foods Correctly

Another serious consideration that is critical to good health and cancer prevention is maintaining the proper acid/alkaline balance. As a result of metabolism the body is constantly generating acid waste products that have to be neutralized in order for the body to maintain its vital life force. When the term pH balance is used, it refers to the "potential" of hydrogen. If any given solution contains many hydrogen ions it is said to be an acid solution. An alkaline solution then would be one containing a small amount of hydrogen ions. All of the tissues and body fluids with the exception of the stomach are alkaline. **The blood pH must always be maintained between a very small range of 7.34 and 7.45.** When the blood is in proper balance it affects and influences proper digestion, which in turn assures the proper assimilation and transportation of nutrients to the cells. This ongoing homeostasis is a delicate design that can be radically affected when our bodies become either too acid or too alkaline. What we eat directly affects the balance of the acid/base balance in our body.

Often people assume that foods like tomatoes or oranges would be acid. This assumption, based on the acidic taste and high concentration of organic acids, doesn't consider the high concentration of alkaline minerals, which produces an overall effect of making the body more alkaline. Basically, foods that contain calcium, magnesium, sodium, potassium and iron will influence alkalinity. These foods are known as alkaline-forming foods. The acid-forming foods contain high concentrations of the minerals sulfur, phosphorous, iodine and chlorine. Although foods contain both acid and alkaline forming minerals it is considered one or the other when it is first burned to its mineral ash in a laboratory and then dissolved in neutral pH water. The water is then tested to find its pH and the result will show how acid- or alkaline-forming each individual food is.

Symptoms of acid excess or acidosis:

Classic symptoms of acidosis are dulled mental abilities, slower mental processing, headaches and depression. Lethargy, fatigue, and muscle tiredness can often occur. When one is low on calcium there can be pain in the lower back and general muscle stiffness as well as leg cramps. The more acid a person is the more they tend towards irritability. They don't call cranky people sour pusses for nothing! As a massage therapist I notice that acid people tend to have sore stiff necks, tense shoulders as well as the tendency towards arthritis. When calcium is low, people experience spasms and twitches. Stomach upset and irritations in the gastric linings of the intestines is an obvious result of too much acid. It is not uncommon to find constipation in acidic people. Many researchers assert that cancer growth is encouraged in an acid system, which makes sense since cancer cells can thrive in an acid state whereas normal cells degenerate. This is precisely why we should aim to eat closer to the alkaline state. It is a delicate balance though, as too much alkalinity presents its own problems.

Symptoms of too much alkalinity:

Extreme nervousness and anxiety or over-excitability are key symptoms when a person is too alkaline. Along with these symptoms people might experience some muscle pains and slowed recovery from injuries. Spaciness is common as is increased nerve sensitivity. Excess alkalinity is when the pH of urine is above 6.3 consistently for a 24-hour period.

Balanced pH characteristics:

- Balanced energy
- Resistance to sickness
- Bowel regularity
- Calm nervous system
- Mental clarity
- General feeling of well-being

A healthy pH range varies from 6.3 to 6.9 and can be checked using special pH paper that checks saliva.

High acid-forming foods:

Cranberries, apple cider vinegar, eggs, flesh foods, fermented foods, walnuts, peanuts.

Acid-forming foods:

Alcohol, medical drugs and synthetic vitamins, cheese, milk, yeast, yogurt, plums, prunes, sugar, most legumes, sodas, sauces like soy sauce, most grains, most nuts, butter, avocado, oils.

Alkaline-forming foods:

Most fruit and veggies, tomatoes, millet, buckwheat, raw cow and goat milk, bean sprouts, string beans, adzuki beans, soy beans, lima beans, onions, soaked almonds, sunflower sprouts, honey.

High alkaline-forming:

Fresh veggie juice, especially carrot/beet, miso, figs, lemons, wheatgrass, barley grass. *Source:* Conscious Eating *by Gabriel Cousens*

Note: An excellent way to help your system become more alkaline is to use the neutralizer made by Masters Miracle. See **www.rawsome.themastersmiracle.com** for more valuable information.

Also see: *The Secrets of pH Concerning Health and Disease* by Mark Cochran, BS, DC, ND, which can be ordered from above website.

Cancer Concerns

One of the reasons I was motivated to write this book was because of all the people around me who were getting cancer. About 12 years ago I attended the funeral of a friend who left behind her eight year old. Then several years ago another friend died of melanoma. My father was next with colon cancer and a couple years later my sister was diagnosed with melanoma. Last year a dear friend was diagnosed with fourth stage melanoma, and then just two weeks later yet another friend told me she had just been diagnosed! There are of course so many people I meet through my work who have or had cancer. The list is endless. Who will be next? How can we learn from those who have forged the cancer path and how can we prevent being on the list?

Much is being discovered all the time. I have seen many people survive their cancers for various reasons. I absolutely believe it is a very personal choice to go alternative and natural vs. traditional medical. Either way, there are pros and cons, but, diet plays an important role in boosting the immune system and helping the body to recover. Once people get over the initial cancer there is always the concern of the cancer returning. It makes no sense to continue with the previous lifestyle and think that the treatment has zapped the cancer forever with no other change required. So even if you choose the medical route you should seriously look at many factors that may have gotten you in the place your body is in now. There is also much recovery that needs to happen as a result of all the drugs, even when the cancer has been removed or gone into remission. Ask any cancer patient what they have to live with permanently as a result of surgery, chemotherapy and/or radiation. It is important to help support the body so it can rest and repair itself in the way it was created to do.

There is much information available from the alternative world and rather than duplicate all that, my best information for you is to send you directly to some extremely helpful websites:

www.cancercontrolsociety.com

www.curezone.com/diseases/cancer/cancer.html.

www.cancervictors.com

www.cancer-coverup.com

One thing I have seen over and over is that juicing, drinking green drinks like barley grass or wheatgrass, and eating plenty of raw organic food all contribute tremendously to the success of alternative cancer treatments. I also believe it is essential to help the body rid itself of old toxins and the putrefying materials that contribute to creating disease. When the body is free of heavy toxins it is more able to take in the good nutrients and have them penetrate into the cell walls. Once the body is free from the burden of having to fight off all the old pollutants and daily added chemicals, it is freed up to function the way God created it to be able to be self-healing. That is why paying attention to colon health and cleansing is so important. Some people cannot imagine ever going to receive a colonic. Even if we don't have cancer, maintaining colon health is of the utmost importance for the overall health and well being of the body. Eating plenty of raw fruits and vegetables, and taking products like Daily Fiber Blend, barley, and spirulina help to support colon health.

A Great Way to Preserve Fresh Juice

This is a great idea I read in a little book called *Living Food Lifestyle* by Elizabeth Miller. If you would like to drink plenty of fresh juice throughout the day but only have time to juice in the morning, this is the best way I've heard of to keep the juice fresh and able to last for 8 to 10 hours. Purchase a stainless steel lined thermos and rinse it out with filtered water. Lay it horizontally in the freezer overnight and fill it all the way to the top the next morning with your fresh juice. Place the lid on tightly, making a seal as the juice will actually overflow as you screw the lid on. This will, in a sense, vacuum-pack the juice and preserve it so you can enjoy it all day. Seal it quickly after each drink, as oxygen is what destroys the nutrition in the juice.

If your juicer is not able to juice wheatgrass but you would love that option, I've got a great tip for you! Try wrapping the wheatgrass blades inside a piece of lettuce. Roll it up like a burrito and stuff it down the chute of your juicer. Some folks say this works better than buying a new juicer!

About Proper Food Combining

The issue about food combining really has to do with enzymes. The body uses different enzymes to digest different types of food. Eating the wrong combinations can cause foods to be retained longer in the stomach, causing them to rot and ferment.

Ideally it is best to eat fruit alone, especially melons. Remember this one: *"Eat melons alone or leave them alone."* If you violate this rule, watch out, you are in for some serious indigestion and gas!

Keep it simple:

Grains, nuts, seeds, and legumes combine well with all veggies.

All veggies do well together.

Swinging veggie/fruits:

Avocados, bell pepper, cucumber, squash and tomatoes can swing either way and be eaten with the fruits listed below or with the veggies listed below.

Fruit	Veggies
Bananas	Broccoli
Berries	Carrots
Citrus	Cauliflower
Pears	Celery
Vine fruit	Chard
	Collards
	Greens
	Lettuce
	Spinach

I have seen more complicated charts on food combining that talk about acid and sub-acid fruit and various other details. This is a simple and easy-to-remember outline, great for those new to this concept. Again, this is one of those opportunities for you to be aware of how foods affect you. Watch for bloating and gas as signs of poor combinations, assimilation and digestion. Headaches, tummy aches, gas pains and spaciness are all signs that can point to the fallout of poor combinations, food sensitivities or allergies. Of course these symptoms can also indicate other issues.

Chewing foods thoroughly is another essential in the process of good assimilation and digestion. Take time to let those digestive juices/enzymes do what they were designed for.

About Sugar

- ☞ Sugar offers no nutritional value and depletes the body of B vitamins, which in turn lowers our resistance to infection as well as causing irritability and even depression.

- ☞ Excess sugar weakens the white blood cells affecting our immune system and its ability to defend against invading germs.

- ☞ Sugar can add to the clogging of arteries and the buildup of cholesterol.

- ☞ Sugar definitely can cause the type of bacteria that leads to tooth decay.

- ☞ Sugar increases the blood fat levels and can lead to obesity.

- ☞ Eating too much sugar can cause blood sugar problems like hypoglycemia and diabetes.

- ☞ Sugar is an acid forming food, which is exactly what cancer patients don't need.

- ☞ When sugar thrives so does candida.

Sugar and Sweetener Substitutes

Raw unfiltered, uncooked agave (see the *Glossary of Ingredients* to find how to order raw agave) is your best sweetener because it is low glycemic. Raw honey, when used sparingly, has many beneficial nutrients. You can also try using fruit juice sweetened organic apricot jam (Trader Joe's sells a nice organic line of jams) or apple juice concentrate to sweeten your recipes. Another wonderful choice is fresh raw dates. Also, using date soak water works well when something calls for a sweet liquid. Often I throw dates in my tea water to sweeten the brew.

All other sweeteners are really depleting to the body. Even though maple syrup and agave nectar are derived from natural sources, they are cooked to make them into a more free flowing liquid state. This alteration can tend to encourage food allergies when combined with other foods, such as whole wheat. Use these other sweeteners very sparingly.

Because of the previously mentioned neurological issues with substitute sweeteners like NutraSweet or anything using aspartame, immediately discontinue usage. Read the book *Excitotoxins, the Taste That Kills* for excellent detailed information on the dangers of this form of sweeteners.

Diabetes and Hypoglycemia

If you find yourself ready to kill if you miss a meal, or experience anxiety attacks when your tank is on empty, then changing your diet is a must! Do you ever feel faint or exhausted or extremely thirsty? These can be symptoms of blood sugar problems.

I have had hypoglycemia for as long as I can remember. Growing up eating Hostess cupcakes sure didn't help. Nor did all those trips to the ice cream and candy stores. Besides the obvious flirtations with heaps of sugar, all those years of downing pizzas, packaged, processed and fast foods set the stage for a very overworked and undernourished pancreas. Finally after years of searching, experimenting, and many, many blood sugar crashes (some incredibly terrifying), I finally have found ways to keep the balance.

I cannot sing the praises of Organic By Nature products enough. The use of their Carob Mint Spirulina as well as Just Barley powder has done wonders to keep my blood sugar stable. If you are dealing with blood sugar issues of any kind, I highly recommend that you visit the website of The Diabetes Resource Center at **www.diabetesresourcecenter.org**.

The following information has been copied from the website of the Diabetes Resource Center with permission from Sandy Corlett, President.

Hypoglycemia

What is Hypoglycemia? Symptoms:

Hypoglycemia occurs when blood sugar (glucose) drops too low and the brain does not get adequate fuel. Insulin-dependent diabetics can experience hypoglycemia if insulin levels are too high. Hypoglycemia can also occur in healthy people if they have consumed a large amount of high glycemic carbohydrates, such as fruit juice. The fruit juice triggers the release of a large amount of insulin, which then pulls too much glucose from the bloodstream, resulting in hypoglycemia. It can occur quickly and, if not treated immediately, a person with hypoglycemia may become unconscious.

What is Blood Sugar?

Blood sugar is basically the fuel that runs the body. It does not build strong, healthy muscles, bones, organs or glands. If a muscle does not have adequate blood sugar it becomes weak. Nerves and the brain depend upon normal sugar levels to function properly. When blood sugar is out of normal balance, many types of symptoms develop because nearly all tissues in the body depend on it to function.

Diabetes is a condition in which the blood sugar level is too high; hypoglycemia is a condition in which the blood sugar is too low. The pancreas secretes insulin to lower and use blood sugar; the adrenal glands and pancreas produce hormones to raise the blood sugar level. In the case of hypoglycemia, if still more sugar is needed, some other adrenal gland hormones convert fat and protein to sugar. In the body's effort to maintain proper blood sugar levels, the glands that regulate it may become stressed and cause symptoms.

Who is at risk?

Everyone who lives and breathes needs to be concerned about hypoglycemia and diabetes. Energy is produced from glucose, and glucose is produced from our food. If we are not eating properly, we are not producing efficient energy. Then we begin storing fat, and we set the stage for illness and disease. Any time one of our basic needs is out of balance, the body is under stress and cannot function properly.

Most people walk around every day in some state of blood sugar imbalance. The symptoms of hypoglycemia and diabetes are a clear indication that the body is not processing or metabolizing glucose properly. The most overlooked symptoms are fatigue, depression, stress and obesity. There is a direct correlation between obesity and insulin insensitivity. However, you do not have to be 50 to 100 lbs. overweight to have blood sugar problems. If you are overweight, you have a 200% greater chance of developing Type II diabetes, which usually manifests itself with hypoglycemia first. Left undiagnosed, untreated and unmanaged, hypoglycemia can turn into diabetes.

Symptoms:

Feeling shaky

Sweating

Dizziness

Weakness and/or overwhelming tiredness

Rapid heartbeat

Numbness or tingling in mouth or lips

Hunger

Other symptoms that may come on more slowly are:

Crying

Irritability and/or anger

Drowsiness

Mental Confusion and/or difficulty in thinking

Poor coordination (may result in trouble walking)

Blurred vision and/or headaches

Slurred speech

Impaired Glucose Tolerance (IGT) affects nearly everyone. The body has either too much or too little insulin. Neither state is healthy. Continuous cycles of roller coaster high and low blood sugar levels can develop into hypoglycemia and diabetes. It can be prevented, managed and controlled. Nearly everyone at some point in their life has experienced low blood sugar (hypoglycemia), they just don't recognize it. They pay more attention to the time of day, weather, and the clothes they are wearing than they do to their body.

Causes:

Some common every day causes of hypoglycemia or low blood sugar are:

Taking too much insulin (diabetics)

Eating at the wrong time

Skipping meals or snacks

Extra exercise without additional food

There are other contributing causes including: improper nutrition, resulting from the over-consumption of processed, chemically treated, overcooked, high fat, high glycemic, packaged fast food and nutrient-deficient food.

Other Causes:

Hyperinsulinism is a condition wherein too much insulin is secreted for the body's needs; thus, the blood sugar level is lowered too far. Sometimes hyperinsulinism can result from something as simple as eating too much sugar rapidly. Foods with high sugar concentration, such as soda, sport drinks, candy, pies and cake may cause a rapid rise in blood sugar. Some people are sensitive to this rapid change, and excessive insulin is secreted, lowering the blood sugar too far. Unfortunately, the individual then wants (or craves) more sugar to bring the blood sugar level up again. A vicious cycle is started with another insulin response. Often the proper treatment for hyperinsulinism is to simply avoid eating foods with high concentrations of refined white sugar.

Functional Hypoadrenia—The adrenal glands are partially responsible for raising the blood sugar level when it is too low. If the blood sugar level is frequently lowered by a condition such as hyperinsulinism, the adrenal glands may eventually become depleted and the blood sugar remains low. This is not complete adrenal failure, which is called Addison's disease and is life-threatening; rather, the adrenal glands are not capable of optimally performing all the functions required of them. The depleted adrenal gland condition, known as functional hypoadrenia, can be the initial cause of a blood sugar handling stress (hypoglycemia). The adrenal glands can become exhausted for many reasons; primary among them is stress. The adrenal glands are very important in handling stress, and may become overworked.

Malabsorption. A type of hypoglycemia is caused by a lack of normal digestive activity in which food is not absorbed and used properly.

Dietary Inadequacy. Often, hypoglycemia is simply the result of inadequate dietary intake. This may happen in weight reduction programs such as the popular low-carbohydrate diet. Also, inadequate fat and/or protein in the diet can contribute to hypoglycemia, because these items are used in forming new sugar in the body when sugar stores are low.

Management:

The first step is to properly evaluate the body for sugar handling problems. Laboratory tests are used to determine if there is a condition of diabetes or disease-caused hypoglycemia. Severe hypoglycemia is usually caused by a pancreatic tumor; however, this is rare. The six-hour glucose tolerance test, used to determine how the body is controlling sugar levels, is recommended, to properly diagnose hypoglycemia. However, home blood glucose testing is the best way to monitor your daily values.

Because the symptoms can be complex and varied among people with hypoglycemia or sugar-handling problems, many doctors do not understand the condition and tend to label the patient "hypochondriac" or "nervous." The suffering individual is given tranquilizers, or given no answer. Occasionally when hypoglycemia is recognized, a diet to include a larger sugar intake is prescribed. Although this temporarily relieves the symptoms, it very often adds fuel to the fire and makes the condition worse.

While most people can eat when and what they want, the hypoglycemic does not have that luxury. Your blood sugar level fluctuates throughout the day with your eating and physical activities. As you take in nourishment, especially sugars, the blood sugar level rises; insulin keeps it from going too high and prevents you from becoming a diabetic. Failure to maintain a balanced nutritional plan of carbohydrates, protein and fat can result in the symptoms of hypoglycemia. (Please see the note below to request the brochure *Hypoglycemia & Nutrition* for treatment and management.)

Complications:

It is important to remember that, like diabetes, hypoglycemia remains a potential life-threatening condition with short-term and long-term complications. For those taking insulin, hypoglycemia or low blood sugar is a constant concern. If the low blood sugar is allowed to go on untreated, you may experience increased confusion and disorientation; difficulty standing or sitting; convulsions or seizures, and unconsciousness.

You may not experience all of these symptoms—low blood sugar affects different people in different ways. You will, however, feel very different from the way you normally feel. Early detection is critical. Remember, uncontrolled hypoglycemia can develop into diabetes.

The GOOD NEWS is: Hypoglycemics can live a normal healthy life with the proper education, nutrition, exercise, stress control, management and treatment. Complications can be delayed, halted and even prevented!

Blood Glucose Testing:

If you experience any of the symptoms, do a blood sugar test to confirm that low blood sugar is the cause of your symptoms. Blood sugar testing is the most important key in taking control of your hypoglycemia (diabetes, IGT) and your life. You cannot rely solely on how you feel—your blood sugar may be higher or lower than normal. You must test your blood sugar to know how well your nutritional management program is working.

Record keeping is important for you and your doctor to see and correct any problems you may be having in controlling your sugar levels. Blood sugars will form a pattern over a period of time. Monitoring is a powerful tool in tracking and controlling your blood sugar levels which will help prevent the development of diabetes and long-term complications.

Is there any hope?

It is important to understand that hypoglycemia, diabetes, and IGT can be prevented, managed and controlled! Remember: hypoglycemia—like diabetes—is a blood sugar handling problem, therefore, we recommend you follow the **7 Steps to Diabetes Management.** For a **free Diabetes-Glucose Screening Test Kit**, and information on diabetes, digestion, nutrition, stress control and more contact:

Diabetes Resource Center
P.O.Box 390397, Snellville, GA 30039
770-982-4190 or 800-354-0004
www.diabetesresourcecenter.org.

Note: The Diabetes Resource Center is grateful to receive contributions to support their ability to reach as many people as possible. Donations enable them to distribute free test kits and other valuable support. If you can help, please see above contact information.

About Weight Loss

Excess weight is a sign of dis-ease in the body. It is a symptom that the body is not able to properly handle the foods ingested. There are usually several factors involved like excess food intake, poor food metabolism, toxic and chemical foods that drag the system down, lack of exercise, blood sugar issues, etc. No matter what the combination of circumstances that led to weight gain, for weight loss to be significant, permanent and healthy, several factors must exist:

First and foremost the body must be detoxified. Years of old toxins are stored in the fat cells. When we ingest foods loaded with preservatives and chemicals, our bodies don't know how to relate to these foreign substances. They aren't like proteins, carbohydrates or fats, so the body either treats them as invaders and works very hard to process and filter them out, or instead these poisons are stored in fat cells. In fact the body manufactures fatty pockets (out of fat cells) to warehouse these peculiar substances. The result of this is very odd-shaped, flabby cellulite bodies that possess fatty rolls to house these unhealthy toxins. Elimination of toxins and the breaking down of fat cells is the key to success. When colonic therapy and juice fasting seem too radical, you might want to try using Daily Fiber Blend, made by Platinum Health Products, adding in a green drink like barley or wheatgrass daily (see whole food supplement section), and eating as close to raw as possible. Using fiber-based products such as Daily Fiber Blend can create a nice jump start on the road to detoxification and elimination. Ideally, though I believe it is best to provide the body with the correct components that grease the wheels, so to speak. With the permission of David Sandoval, creator of Organic By Nature products, to use information from a portion of a tape lecture he gave concerning the value of green foods, I want to expand on what I am saying:

"Now, many people talk about the need to eliminate properly and they discuss fiber. But did you know that we need potassium and cell salts in order to create an environment that eliminates toxins from the body? You see, potassium causes the bowel to contract and sodium causes the bowel to expand. So, when you take green foods which create abundant potassium and cell salts in the environment where the intestines contract and expand, then proper elimination can take place. If we only take fiber as a means of increasing our elimination, then we can actually suffer by bulking up and bulking up and literally stretching the bowel, stretching the skin of the intestines. It is only through eating these green foods that have both potassium and cell salts that we create the environment of contraction and expanding that leads to proper elimination on a daily basis of accumulated waste in the bowel; so it's not just fiber, it is also trace minerals which lead to proper elimination."

Drinking plenty of purified water gives the body a way to eliminate old toxic material. Next, cravings have to be addressed. Adding foods rich in chromium can help decrease food cravings. Foods such as brewer's yeast, apples, whole grains and some sea foods can make an impact. Drinking green drinks as well as fresh vegetable juices can provide much needed cell nutrition, offering the body vital nutrients it has been starving for. Once these nutrients are delivered, the cravings quiet down tremendously.

By eating vitamin and mineral rich complex carbohydrates, continual hunger can be curtailed. Often when people start eating a mostly raw diet they find that their hunger vanishes and they experience a new sense of being nourished which leads to eating satisfaction.

As we get older, the issue of metabolism gets stronger! We have to find ways to take in foods that our bodies can process, use and burn in the most efficient way. When our bodies are burdened or not able to digest food properly this can cause various metabolic processes that can lead to weight gain. Exercise plays an important role in metabolism as well as providing a way to encourage the body to work synergistically to eliminate toxins and waste materials.

Paying close attention to foods that cause reactions and eliminating them will greatly increase your ability to be successful. One way to perceive a food sensitivity is to take your pulse prior to eating and then 30, 60 and 90 minutes later. Keeping a food journal, tracking all foods eaten daily, and documenting any altered pulse rates can be a tremendous tool for getting a grasp on what is working and what isn't. This also gives you a good reality check on the quantity of food ingested daily.

One of the best food discoveries and weight loss secrets I have found is spirulina. Once again with the permission of David Sandoval of Organic By Nature, I would like to quote to you his information concerning spirulina and weight loss.

(Edited from *Power Health with Spirulina—Nature's Richest Whole Food*, an educational guide by Pure Planet Products, Inc.):

"Losing weight, or more specifically, body fat, can be a source of frustration to those changing their eating habits. This is largely due to a lack of knowledge about body chemistry, and the various ways the body stores and uses nutrition, especially as it relates to the accumulation, use and storage of fat.

Though decreasing food intake may lower overall weight, cutting calories alone does not maintain muscle tissue nor does it reverse the altered chemistry of the muscles, nor does it permanently keep the body from resuming its previous fat set point. In fact, a weight loss quick-fix attacks subcutaneous fat first and will remove intramuscular fat only under the most severe circumstances. To instruct the body to undergo such rigor would be disappointing at best because nothing prevents weight gain once again. Radical dieting, unbalanced eating, shots and fasting can worsen the situation because they have been shown to lessen muscle mass as the person is losing fat.

How does the body respond to all of this? The body's first reaction is to draw on the energy that is immediately available in any emergency. This is not fat; the body has no means to make immediate use of stored fat. The body's immediately available form of energy is a substance called glycogen which is a form of glucose (a carbohydrate) stored with water in the muscles and in the body's most metabolically active vital organ, the liver.

For many years it was assumed that the glycogen stored in the liver was the principal source of blood sugar between meals. However, more recently it has been shown that this glycogen is hoarded by the liver. Instead of giving up its glycogen for blood sugar, the liver converts protein to glucose. This means that if the body were to subsist on a starvation diet, it would actually convert valuable body protein to blood sugar as fuel for the brain.

Spirulina is the only plant food that contains glycogen. Glycogen is not ordinarily available through our diet. Muscles store glycogen and use it as a principal source of both immediate and long-term energy. The more glycogen available during intense or sustained exercise, the greater the potential for improved functioning. When glycogen levels drop, weakness and fatigue set in rapidly. Spirulina shortcuts the metabolic process of synthesizing glycogen from our food and supplies it directly pre-formed, thus sparing the body's own glycogen reserves.

The amount of fat that we might gain is not genetically pre-ordained, but determined by our chosen lifestyles. When a person reaches adult weight, the body establishes the enzyme system, hormone levels, and musculoskeletal pattern to remain at that weight. Whatever amount of fat one maintains for a period of a year or more then becomes the body's reference point. From then on all body systems will be geared to that reference or fat set point. The body protects its fat cells against invasion and deprivation just as it protects all other cells, so if overweight for a year or more, the body demands to be kept at this set point.

Exercise is a key component that can successfully help reset the body's set point. Daily exercise, such as aerobic, brisk walking, where the lungs are breathing deeply and the heart is working vigorously, forms a central part of permanent fat loss. This is true for two major reasons: first, regular aerobic exercise stimulates metabolism, which in itself helps burn fat, and second, such exercise encourages the rapid and efficient elimination of toxicity from the system through the breath, the skin (in the form of sweat), the bowels and the kidneys. It even improves the functions of the liver, which is absolutely central to solving the problem of excess fat-stores in the body.

"Old habits are broken not by self-coercion, but by attraction to new habits that give an awakened sense of aliveness."

–D. Sandoval

A key factor to explain why some people lose weight while some seem to maintain normal weight effortlessly is the efficiency of special tissue in the back of the neck and along the spine, called brown adipose tissue or brown fat. Unlike ordinary yellow fat, brown fat has a very high metabolic response to any excess calories consumed, by burning them off as body heat rather than storing them as fat. Unfortunately, many overweight people suffer from under-active brown fat.

A number of factors are known to contribute to the activation of brown fat. Interestingly, the essential fatty acid (EFA) content of body fat is inversely proportional to body weight. This means that the higher the level of EFA's in the body, the lower the body weight, and vice versa.

At the University of Wales in Cardiff, studies indicate that gamma linoleic acid (GLA) has a stimulating effect on brown fat tissue. The prostaglandins, which are the end products of GLA metabolism, possibly accelerate the mitochondria activity of the brown fat. There is no better food source of GLA readily available than spirulina.

Spirulina also contains phenylalanine which is a natural appetite suppressant. Phenylalanine, an amino acid, produces a chemical known as cholecystokinin which in turn acts quickly on the appetite center of the hypothalamus in the brain. This helps suppress appetite. Spirulina is one of the most easily assimilated forms of protein, keeping blood sugar at the correct level and preventing hunger pangs.

Taking six to ten tablets of 100% pure spirulina on an empty stomach one half hour before meals is an effective and beneficial method for weight loss.

Spirulina is an exceptionally rich source of arginine, an amino acid that releases growth hormone (Gh). Gh is a polypeptide hormone that is secreted by the pituitary gland. Gh stimulates the body's own regenerative process by increasing the rate of protein synthesis. It causes muscle cells to grow and multiply by directly increasing the rate at which amino acids enter the muscles and are built up into protein. Gh promotes fat burning, causing cells to switch from burning carbohydrates to burning fat for energy. It stimulates fat tissues to release stored fat and it stimulates other cells to break down the released fat molecules.

With a desire to decrease body fat, one must increase lean muscle tissue and muscle enzymes through exercising and ensuring that the diet contains branched chain amino acids (BCAA's) for muscle biosynthesis. Three BCAA's, leucine, isoleucine and valine, provide more than 70% of all the free nitrogen to the body and regulate muscle protein synthesis. Even if one is sedentary, 90% of all the calories burned are burned by the muscles. Specialized enzymes existing only in muscle tissue can increase fat burning by fifty-fold during exercise. Eating the three BCAA's will supply fuel and be converted into glucose for energy when you have high energy demands and diminishing blood sugar levels. If dietary BCAA's are lacking, the body will break down its own muscle tissue resulting in loss of lean muscle mass, lowered metabolism and increased fat deposition.

Spirulina is nature's richest source of BCAA's. It is important to eat as much live or biogenic food as possible. The word biogenic means life-generating, and it refers to living, enzyme-rich, raw foods. Living foods have special properties for both weight loss and high-level health. Fresh fruits (organic whenever possible), sprouted seeds and grains have the highest complement of vitamins and minerals, essential fatty acids, easily assimilated top quality protein, fiber and wholesome carbohydrates. Such a natural complement of nutrients in superbly balanced form supplies the body with substances it needs to function at a high level of efficiency. This is what one wants in order to encourage steady and permanent fat loss.

Discovering spirulina and learning how to use it can awaken a deeper interest in a more natural diet through its powerful rejuvenating effects. Its super nutrition satisfies hunger because it completely meets the body's biochemical needs.

The use of spirulina can help re-establish normal sodium/potassium and acid/alkaline balance. Excess fat and water are reduced, returning the body to a leaner, better balance. The change is gentle, indirect and stable. Old habits are broken not by self-coercion, but by attraction to new habits that give an awakened sense of aliveness. This long-term subtle approach along with regular exercise and appropriate supplementation enables one to successfully stay lean and healthy."

How To Cook Legumes

We just talked about spirulina, which is a superior way to get quality, easily digestible protein, especially in a vegan diet. Another choice, especially for those wanting to eat less animal products, is with beans. I use two methods for cooking beans. In both cases one must carefully pick through the beans, removing little pebbles, debris and discolored pieces. All legumes except for lentils, split peas and black-eyed peas require soaking. The benefit of soaking is twofold: 1) to reduce cooking time, and 2) to reduce intestinal gas (as beans are often very difficult to digest, you may find it necessary to use digestive enzymes).

Method I

Place legumes in a large bowl and cover with three times as much filtered cool water. Soak overnight on the counter top. Drain, rinse well and cook in fresh filtered water or veggie broth.

Method II

Place legumes in large stockpot with three times as much filtered water and boil for five minutes. Turn off heat and let soak as is for one hour. Drain, rinse, and cook in fresh water or veggie broth. When cooking legumes I like to add pieces of cut up kombu and garlic salt, and often I throw in a tsp. of cumin.

Once the water has come to a boil, reduce heat to low and simmer with the lid on until the beans are very soft. Wait until after the beans are cooked to add Celtic Sea Salt, otherwise they may not soften properly.

Legume – 1 C Soaked	Water	Cooking Time	Yield
Adzuki beans	3 cups	1½ hours	2 cups
Black beans	1 quart	1½ hours	2 cups
Black eyed peas	3 cups	1 hour	2 cups
Garbanzos (*soaked overnight*)	1 quart	3 hours	2 cups
Great Northern beans	3½ cups	2 hours	2 cups
Kidney beans	3 cups	1½ hours	2 cups
Lentils & split peas	3 cups	45 minutes	2¼ cups
Pinto beans	3 cups	1½ hours	2 cups
Small white beans	3 cups	1½ hours	2 cups
Soybeans	1 quart	3–4 hours	2 cups

The Hazards of Using a Microwave

In a nutshell, the use of microwaves violently deforms the molecular structure of foods. Dr. Lita Lee, in her book called *Health Effects of Microwave Radiation—Microwave Ovens*, has stated that every microwave oven leaks electromagnetic radiation. She feels that every substance cooked in a microwave converts it to a "dangerous organ-toxic and carcinogenic product."

I have been granted permission to copy the following information, which I found at an interesting website. For more in depth information I highly recommend that you visit this site yourself at: **www.healthfree.com/paa/paa0001.htm.**

"From the conclusions of the Swiss, Russian and German scientific clinical studies, we can no longer ignore the microwave oven sitting in our kitchens. Based on this research, we will conclude this article with the following: *Ten Reasons to Throw Out Your Microwave Oven.*

1) Continually eating food processed from a microwave oven causes long-term permanent brain damage by "shorting out" electrical impulses in the brain (de-polarizing or de-magnetizing the brain tissue).

2) The human body cannot metabolize (break down) the unknown by-products created in microwaved food.

3) Male and female hormone production is shut down and/or altered by continually eating microwaved foods.

4) The effects of microwaved food by-products are residual (long term, permanent) within the human body.

5) Minerals, vitamins, and nutrients of all microwaved food are reduced or altered so that the human body gets little or no benefit, or the human body absorbs altered compounds that cannot be broken down.

6) The minerals in vegetables are altered into cancerous free radicals when cooked in microwave ovens.

7) Microwaved foods cause stomach and intestinal cancerous growths (tumors). This may explain the rapidly increasing rate of colon cancer in America.

8) The prolonged eating of microwaved foods causes cancerous cells to increase in human blood.

9) Continual ingestion of microwaved food causes immune system deficiencies through lymph gland and blood serum alterations.

10) Eating microwaved food causes loss of memory, concentration, emotional instability and decrease of intelligence.

Have you tossed out your microwave oven yet? "

What About Eating at Restaurants?

In the rapid pace of our culture, eating at restaurants is a fact of life. However, did you stop and think about another fact concerning restaurant eating? Most restaurants use microwaves to prepare some portion of the meals they serve. Most sauces and salad dressings (when they aren't made from scratch) contain hidden MSG. The more delicious the food tastes, the more you can bet food additives, colorings, preservatives, highly processed salt, tons of sugar, etc. are sure to be found. So what to do? Relax and simply make the best choices you can.

I like to carry my own salad dressing in a small glass jar that I can fit in my purse. I also bring my own water in a stainless steel thermos, when possible. Ask if the food you are interested in is microwaved. Eat simply, but most of all try to enjoy your time out.

My biggest vice in life is eating at restaurants. Before I got my current education on food, nutrition and healthy choices I ate out at least twice a week without a care in the world; bite after bite oblivious to what I was ingesting, like millions of people every day! Now I find the power of information has transformed my eating habits on many levels, especially at restaurants. I find that as my palate has changed, the kind of restaurants I choose has also. In this natural evolution, I find I'm gracefully attracted to ordering differently. As my own cooking or "uncooking" has evolved and I have found such satisfaction from the foods I eat, I find that when I do eat out, foods taste too salty or too sweet, or too oily, or too heavy. The desire to go out is less and less. It all gets much simpler over time!

About Salt

It has become apparent that table salt as we have known it is not on the must-get list. We all know that packaged foods contain tons of it, and there is the heavy-handed use of it at restaurants. One thing many folks don't realize is that when the words "sea salt" are used on supposed health food packages it doesn't mean that this salt is any better. This salt usually has gone through a process of being mechanically harvested from dirt or concrete basins. Then it is put through several artificial processes and heated to the point of altering its molecular structure. This robs the salt of its essential minerals. The salt is further assaulted when chemical additives are used to make it free flowing, bleached to make it pure white, and iodized! Celtic Sea Salt, Real Salt, and my current favorite salt, Stardust Ra Sea Salt from The Whole Food Farmacy (because they even remove microscopic dirt particles) are the only salts to use. It is best to look for salts like these that have been hand-raked and dried by the sun, and are filled with valuable minerals. Real Salt is mined from the earth in Utah and can be found at health food stores, or check www.realsalt.com. Stardust Ra Sea Salt can be ordered by going to www.rawsome.wholefoodfarmacy.com.

Some people feel that all salt should be discarded. One of the best forms of naturally-occurring salt in the correct mineral balance can be found in celery. It is wise to drink celery juice often and add it to other vegetable juices.

Quick check nutrient value and benefits of whole foods from A–Z:

Apples – high in soluble fibers, especially pectin good for lowering cholesterol

Apricots – rich source of beta-carotene, iron, and potassium, high in fiber

Artichokes – good source of folate, vitamin C and potassium, high in fiber

Asparagus – folate, vitamins A and C

Avocados – folate, vitamin A and potassium, good protein, iron, magnesium and vitamins C, E, and B6

Bananas – potassium, folate, and vitamins C and B6

Bean Sprouts – folate, good source of protein, vitamin C, B and iron

Beets – folate and vitamin C

Beet greens – rich source of potassium, calcium, iron, beta-carotene and vitamin C

Blackberries – vitamin C and bioflavinoids, folate, vitamin E, iron and calcium as well as anticancer chemicals

Blueberries – dietary fiber, some vitamin C and iron, may prevent some urinary tract infections, protects against some intestinal upsets

Broccoli – excellent source of vitamin C, good source of vitamin A and folate, significant protein, calcium, iron and other important minerals, bioflavinoids, high in fiber, protects against cancer

Brussels sprouts – excellent source of vitamin C, protein, folate, vitamin A, iron and potassium, bioflavinoids and protects against cancer

Buckwheat –iron, magnesium, protein and fiber

Cabbage – excellent source of vitamin C, high in fiber, may help prevent colon cancer and malignancies stimulated by estrogen, juice helps peptic ulcers

Carrots – beta-carotene, dietary fiber and potassium, may protect against cancer, helpful with night blindness

Cauliflower - excellent source of vitamin C, folate, and potassium, high in fiber

Celery – high fiber, potassium, possible cancer protection

Cherries – vitamin C, high in pectin fiber that reduces cholesterol

Coconuts – useful source of iron and fiber, easy to digest high fatty acids mainly comprised of lauric acid known for its immune building properties

Corn – folate, thiamine, vitamins A and C, potassium and iron

Cranberries – vitamin C and fiber, bioflavinoids helpful in preventing cancer, juice helps urinary tract infections

Cucumbers – good roughage, some folate and vitamin C

Currants – vitamin C and potassium, high in bioflavinoids

Dates – excellent potassium, iron and calcium, high in fiber

Figs – rich in magnesium, potassium, calcium and iron plus high in fiber

Grapefruits – high vitamin C and potassium, fair amount of folate, iron, calcium, red kind has beta-carotene, high fiber, bioflavinoids to protect against heart disease and cancer

Grapes – fair amount of iron, potassium and vitamin C, high pectin and bioflavinoids

Guavas – great source of vitamin C, high in pectin, potassium and iron

Kiwi – best source of vitamin C in a fruit, good on potassium and fiber

Leeks – vitamin C and small amounts of niacin and calcium

Legumes – the most protein from a plant derived food, good source of B complex, iron, potassium, zinc, and soluble fiber

Lemons – great source of vitamin C

Lettuce and salad greens (except iceberg) – some types have high beta-carotene, folate, vitamin C, calcium, iron and potassium

Limes – vitamin C

Mangoes – beta-carotene and vitamin C, E and niacin, high in potassium, iron and fiber

Melons – yellow ones high in vitamin A, most are a good source of vitamin C and potassium, some high in pectin

Mushrooms – various varieties are rich in minerals and some are high in glutamic acid which boost immune function (like shiitakes)

Nectarines – beta-carotene and potassium, some vitamin C, high in pectin fiber

Nuts and seeds – rich source of vitamin E and potassium, most high in minerals including calcium, iron, magnesium and zinc. Some provide B vitamins, others folate and niacin. Great source of protein.

Oranges – vitamin C, beta-carotene, folate, thiamine and potassium

Papayas – great vitamins A and C plus potassium, also used as a digestive enzyme

Parsnips – high in fiber, some vitamin C, folate, and potassium

Peaches – vitamins A, C and potassium, plus dietary fiber

Pears – good vitamin C and folate, dietary fiber

Peas and pods – vitamins A and C, thiamine, riboflavin, potassium and high pectin fiber

Peppers – vitamins A and C

Pineapples – vitamin C with some vitamin B6, folate, thiamine, iron and magnesium

Plums – vitamin C, riboflavin, some B vitamins and potassium

Potatoes – vitamins C and B6, and potassium

Prunes – nice source of vitamin A, great in B vitamins, E, potassium, and iron

Pumpkins – beta-carotene, vitamin C and potassium, high in fiber

Pumpkin seeds – nice source of protein, iron, B vitamins, vitamin E and fiber

Radishes – vitamin C and high in fiber

Raspberries – high in vitamin C, folate, iron and potassium, provides bioflavinoids, high in fiber

Rice – some varieties provide B vitamins and iron and when combined with beans provides a nice form of protein

Seaweed – may provide an excellent source of iodine, calcium, copper, iron, magnesium and potassium with some varieties high in vitamins B, C and beta-carotene as well as good usable source of protein

Spinach – rich in vitamin A and folate, nice source of vitamin C and potassium, provides vegetarians with a nice plant protein, as well as great antioxidants and bioflavinoids that help block cancer-causing substances

Squash – summer varieties provide some folate and vitamins A and C while winter squash are rich in vitamins A and C, folate and potassium

Strawberries – excellent in vitamin C, good folate, potassium and anticancer bioflavinoids as well as good fiber

Tangerines – vitamin C, beta-carotene and potassium, pectin fiber

Tomatoes – helpful source of vitamins A and C, folate, and potassium as well as antioxidant called lycopene that protects against some cancers

Turnips – vitamin C and some calcium and potassium plus dietary fiber

Watercress – beta-carotene, vitamins A and C, calcium, iron and potassium, as well as antioxidants preventing cancer

Yams – rich in beta-carotene, good source of vitamins C and B6, folate, potassium and high in fiber

Zucchini – provides vitamins A, C and folate

Source: This information has been compiled from various research as well as information cross-referenced from *Reader's Digest Foods That Harm, Foods That Heal*, 1997

Raw!

***Raw, raw, raw.* Why eat raw?** *Sis, boom bah?*

Well…because dear **Sis**/ters out there, it seems as though, if you find yourself as a wife or mother, one of our callings is to provide nourishment for our families. (This applies to men and dads out there too!) If that nourishment we provide comes to our families from us as microwaved, processed, artificial, chemically thriving, over salted, overcooked, oily food, then guess what? We are helping to lower the **boom** on our families. Do not forget that this type of food is dead food. All food that is cooked past 117° destroys all enzymes, and enzymes are what feed and nourish every cell in our bodies.

Bah! Are we to be blind sheep led to the slaughter following the way of the world eating man-made, nutrient-starved, and depleted foods? Are we to go around blindly being led by our taste buds? Do we want to go around unconsciously not having any concern for how we care for our God-given bodies?

> *All food that is cooked past 117° destroys all enzymes, and enzymes are what feed and nourish every cell in our bodies.*

What is all this talk about enzymes? Is this yet another food fad? Enzymes are what eating raw is all about. Enzymes are foundational for proper body functioning. **Put simply, no enzymes, no life!** The more enzymes, the more life. Enzymes are found in every cell of anything that lives. They are composed of amino acids, which are the structural units of all proteins. Enzymes are catalysts in the metabolic process. They jump-start chemical reactions responsible for building up new tissue growth as well as breaking down substances, as in digestion. Because enzymes have so many applications in body processes, we contain over three thousand kinds of enzymes, with each enzyme performing a different job. They are like construction workers busy building and repairing parts of our bodies. Enzymes are so key to our well-being that when the quantities decrease there is a noticeable decrease in health as well. Injury, illness, stress and aging all play a role in decreasing the amount and potency of enzymes.

Because enzymes are very sensitive to heat, it is critical to eat food in a non-heated, thus non-deadened state. Live raw food, like sprouts, provide the best source of enzymes. Next best would be raw organic juices. To experience more vitality, energy and aliveness in your body, simply decrease cooked and dead food and replace with live raw food.

The first function of enzymes is to help break down our ingested food. But what if the food you just ingested was cooked food? Then you are asking your body to provide existing enzymes for this purpose, which causes a deficit from your body's cells.

As we grow older, the body begins to produce considerably fewer enzymes due to the aging process. This is why we see elderly people having more of a challenge digesting and processing their food as each year passes. As long as people keep eating dead food they can expect to have the related problems that go with enzyme depletion. Remember then, that adding enzyme-rich foods to your diet helps to prevent robbing your body of these vital life-giving elements.

Asking your body to supply the enzymes means creating an unnecessary task that is wearing over time. This can result in a lack of energy, digestive ailments, chronic illness and disease. The first thing I hear people say once they have been on a mostly raw diet for as little as one week is: "I can't believe how much more energy I have!" Cooked food creates more waste by-products and toxins that the body has to work harder to try to eliminate. If optimum health is what you are after, then eating mostly raw will take you there.

Letting go of sugar and caffeine is a huge step. I know the thought of not having that stimulation is scary for people who depend on it to make it through their day. However, you really will be pleasantly surprised to find that once you make it through the first week on a mostly raw food diet, you will begin to experience real energy. The restored vitality, alertness, and spunk that come from eating this way more than makes up for what you are letting go of.

After about three weeks, sugar stops calling you and real food takes on new flavors and meaning. You will find that your body's cravings will disappear and you will know satisfaction from the nourishment your body is receiving. Eating a piece of fruit will become a simple yet fulfilling dessert. You can still allow yourself the opportunity to enjoy sweet, rawsome "special treats" once in awhile. What emerges then is a nice sense of what "special occasions" mean.

If eating all raw seems too overwhelming for you, then try gradually shifting to whole, organic foods, adding more and more raw into your meals. Eating raw until supper and then adding about 20 percent cooked at dinner is a wonderful goal to work toward.

RAW RAW RAW SIS BOOM BAH—YOU CAN DO IT!

Recommended Reading on Enzymes:

Food Enzymes For Health & Longevity by Howell

Food Enzymes by Tonita d'Raye

Enzyme Nutrition by Howell

Food Enzymes—The Missing Link to Radiant Health by Santillo

The Complete Book of Enzyme Therapy by Dr. Anthony Cichoke

References:

Grossman, et al. *The Effect of Dietary Composition on the Pancreatic Enzymes.* The American Journal of Physiology. 140:676-682; 1943.

Howell, Edward. *Enzyme Nutrition—The Food Enzyme Concept.* Avery Publishing Group Inc., 1985.

Prochaska and Piekutowski. *On the Synergistic Effects of Enzymes in Food with Enzymes in the Human Body.* A Literature Survey and Analytical Report. Medical Hypotheses 42 (June): 335-362: 1993.

RawSome Kids!

"Train up a child in the way he should go; and when he is old, he will not depart from it" (Proverbs 22:6 NIV).

Raising rawsome kids is definitely going to take some effort on your part, especially if they have always known "foods" like sodas, boxed crackers, chips, candy and fast foods. I've heard it before. Moms whining: "You don't know my children, they will never eat that!" Well guess what? You taught them how to eat that every time you ate that way or served it to them. The good news is that you can re-teach/train them the right way by what you eat, what you buy and serve them, and how you educate them.

Maybe it is time to sit your children down and say that you have made a mistake. Let them know how much you love and care about them. Tell them that their health and safety is not only your job as their parent but also your heart's concern. With so much talk about various impending diseases or outbreaks the best thing we can do is to keep building our immune systems.

Many people in alternative health don't see sickness as the result of invading germs. The "wash your hands so you don't spread germs" theory is just bunk to many. Instead, the thinking is that healthy immune systems don't attract pathogens in the first place. Think of it like this. If a dog comes by and dumps over a trash can filled with rotting food pretty soon the bugs will crawl, walk, run and fly on over for the feast! If you come along and clean up the waste site then the bugs pass on by, as there is nothing to attract them anymore. I know this is a rather simplistic idea in regards to illness but I do believe this attempts to explain why some people get the flu when others don't, even though the exposure has been the same.

Feeding our kids as much raw, organic fruits and veggies as possible is our best weapon against invading factors. Of course, there is so much in their lives that we cannot control, but we certainly want to contribute as much as possible to the enhancement of their immune systems. The immune system is our front line of defense. We need to support it, encourage it and actively uplift it daily.

The best and easiest way to impact your child's immune system daily is to feed and nourish their cells with fresh organic juice made with a high quality juicer like the Visor or the Champion juicer. The next best thing would be to add sprouted food to their diets. As mentioned earlier in the book, this type of food is still living and provides the maximum enzymes.

The main things active, growing children need in their diets are proteins, carbohydrates and fats. Plenty of them in a nice wide range of colors, tastes and textures. This will assure them all the vitamins and minerals they need. Because kids are bursting with energy and expending large quantities of it, they need frequent quality refueling. Carbs are good but in the right amounts, and quality counts. If you allow your child to eat massive amounts of toast, then they will actually be creating a sugar addiction even though they aren't ingesting sugar.

Carbs turn to sugar in our body, and this is not the best form of fuel for their tanks. Instead, upgrade to quality carbs. Some bread and butter is not a bad snack, especially if the bread is from sprouted grains as is the case with Ezekiel bread. Encourage them to make shakes using dates as the sweetener and almond butter to add protein. Throw in bananas for the best source of potassium.

There are certain nutrients that kids need in large amounts. One of these is the essential fatty acids (review in the whole foods section of the book). Butter is also an essential for kids. One trick I've learned is that almost anything tastes good with butter. When I first made raw angel hair pasta out of zucchini, I melted butter and garlic to pour over it and Molly hardly noticed the pasta was raw!

Below is a list of nutrients children need in large amounts and some ideas on what foods contain them:

Calcium

Almonds, beans, broccoli, celery, goat cheese and yogurt, goat milk, nuts and seeds (raw unsalted, tahini and other nut butters and nut milks) and greens, especially turnip and collard greens

Iron

Apricots, barley, brown rice, seaweed, black strap molasses, oatmeal, prunes, pumpkin seeds, lentils, baked potatoes, kidney beans, pinto beans, black beans, pumpkin and split peas

Vitamin D

Sun, sun, sun and more fun in the sun! Salmon and some fatty fish, enriched rice milk, granola and bran flakes

Zinc

Asparagus, adzuki beans, brazil nuts, collard greens, kelp, okra, spinach and wheat germ

Omega 3 and Omega 6 Fatty Acid Blend

I like to give Molly two teaspoons a day of Udo's Oil or Pacific Hemp Supreme 7 Oil Blend. Either oil hides easily in the *Sunrise Smoothie** or I use the oil in *Mock Ranch** dressing (*see index for recipes).

Presentation is very important. Find ways to make it fun. By involving your kids in the process, you can come along way fast. Molly came up with the idea of having a salad bar every Monday night. I encourage her to help me set up and help create special decorations to make the servings come alive. For example, we make little mice out of radishes and display them on top of the lettuce-filled salad bowl!

When I make fresh almond milk, she loves to help me squeeze the liquid through the nut bag. I make it a treat for her to get to help, and therefore her enthusiasm follows! She is also very enthusiastic when it comes to making banana ice cream in the Champion juicer. Making fresh juice is another great way to involve the kids. They love to push the fresh fruit and veggie slices through the chute and watch it turn to juice. There are so many ways to involve kids in the kitchen with this type of food preparation. Making homemade popsicles is another example.

The earlier you train them in good eating habits the better, but it is never too late to change! My seventy-five year-old mom learned to make almond milk this year and enjoys using it in place of milk. From kids to grandparents we can all have fun learning, making, and eating the RawSome way!

To me, the words "RawSome Kids" mean teaching and training your kids to eat a diet of mostly raw, some organic cooked, and possibly some quality animal protein foods. (It is recommended that only all-natural, hormone-free, organic and free-range animal products be used). When you raise your children to eat this way, watch them grow and flourish. The less cooked and animal products, the more vitality, health and well-being you will notice.

So many children today suffer from mild to severe learning difficulties. My daughter has dyslexia and auditory processing issues. It is so clear to me how she changes when she eats denatured foods. The main thing I notice when she eats a healthy, life-giving diet is that her moods stay more even and pleasant, and she is calmer and can focus better.

I cannot say enough how important it is for children with learning differences of this type, as well as ADD and ADHD, to stay away from food additives (especially MSG), phosphates, sulfates, enhancers, artificial sweeteners, food dyes, sugar, caffeine, alcohol, packaged and processed foods, denatured foods, microwaved foods, fast foods and sodas. These children especially need high quality essential fatty acids, butter, quality protein and corrective amino acids. *Control Hyperactivity and A.D.D. Naturally* by Billie Jay Sahley, Ph.D. is an excellent book detailing the role of amino acids in the treatment of ADD.

When I was involved in Team Action, a ministry with street kids, I noticed that a large percentage of them had learning differences and had slipped through the cracks. They were told or made to feel that they were stupid and with that came a plummeting sense of self worth. The issues of these kids don't concern just their families (if they are concerned in the first place!). These troubled youth are a societal issue. With the low self-esteem often comes drugs and promiscuous behavior. These kids scramble to eat whatever they can, which only enhances their hard-to-handle symptoms. The surprising factor was finding kids on the streets who didn't fit what I thought would be the norm. I found kids from all walks of life out there and more kids from upper middle class families than one might think. Diet is a huge factor for helping these kids, as is staying away from drugs and alcohol.

I also believe another reason we are seeing such huge statistics of children with learning differences these days has to do with all the drugs taken in the previous generations. I'm not just talking about recreational drugs. I'm talking about the chemicals and drugs that my generation grew up on. I was given Demerol at age 10 because of migraines. I was raised on cough medicines, aspirins, decongestants and a large range of fast and frozen foods. (Have you noticed how many drugs of this sort have been recalled as of late due to such shocking side effects as strokes, seizures and death!?)

The toxic bodies of these children's parents, I believe, set the stage for creating children with brains that aren't wired up and firing correctly. Of course there are many factors to consider and diet and drugs are not the only issues with these children.

When trying to combat such difficult disorders as ADD or ADHD, there has been quite a lot of success with the natural and alternative approach. Although the use of Ritalin is quite popular as prescribed by many respected doctors, there are many serious risks involved (as is true with taking any drug). Ritalin is a class 2 controlled substance. This puts this drug in the same category as cocaine, codeine, morphine and amphetamines. Some of its potential side effects are nervousness and insomnia, anorexia and nausea, blood pressure fluctuations, dizziness, headache, drowsiness, abdominal pain, dermatitis and other skin rashes, motor tics and depression.

If Ritalin is stopped too quickly, or if it is gradually decreased and stopped, it is possible that it can cause fatigue, disturbed sleep, depression, Tourette's Syndrome, psychosis or in extreme cases, suicide. It is critical to work with qualified professionals, especially when beginning or terminating the use of Ritalin!

Choosing what is best for your child is a complicated and involved process. It requires research, education, trial and error, time and experience to make the best decision. There is a time and a place for drugs and supplements, and those choices are very personal. If you find yourself choosing drugs or supplements, diet still has an important role. The role of diet has often been completely ignored or scoffed at by some medical authorities. However, there are countless testimonies from observant parents pointing to the very important role that diet plays in ADD/ADHD and in many other health problems.

It is very evident that there are many children diagnosed and prescribed medications who really don't require them. Often symptoms that seem to be labeled ADD/ADHD actually are a result of other imbalances. For example, when there is a deficiency of enzymes, vitamins, minerals and amino acids, an imbalance is created that disrupts the proper functions of the body and mind. A deficiency or imbalance can bring about poor health that may manifest itself as an inability to concentrate, fatigue or irritability.

Other reasons that may inhibit learning, focus, mood and concentration are:

Food & Environmental Allergies

Typically when the word "allergy" comes up we think of the common symptoms that are overt, like itchy eyes, runny noses and hives. However, there is another form that is more covert and not so easily understood and recognized, as well as being controversial. Symptoms can show up in any part of the body, from headaches, fatigue, inability to concentrate or inability to fall asleep to joint pains, bed-wetting, ear infections, hypoglycemia or ADHD. Various culprits can cause these types of symptoms, the most common ones being cow's milk, wheat, soy, corn and artificial coloring. Other known culprits are dust mites, molds, fungus, and even the family pets! *Is This Your Child* by Dr. Doris Rapp is an excellent book about food allergies, including information on supplementations for ADD/ADHD.

The Yeast Puzzle Piece

Balancing the "friendly bacteria" with other bacteria and yeast in our body is another piece of the health and well-being puzzle. Just ask anyone who has suffered with candida how important this balance is! Factors upsetting this important balance include eating too much refined carbohydrates or taking ANTIBIOTICS. Antibiotics kill off the good bacteria in the gut. The antibiotics don't affect the yeast but without the good bacteria the balance is disrupted, leading to an excess of yeast that produces toxins.

The symptoms may include headaches, inability to concentrate, a spacy "foggy-headedness," depression, mood swings, hyperactivity etc. These symptoms often overlap those of food allergies. Candida can definitely be controlled through proper diet, which has largely to do with eliminating all sugar, yeast, alcohol and fermented foods.

There are many good books available on candida. *Help for the Hyperactive Child* by Dr. William Crook, M.D. is an excellent book on the subject.

Another helpful guide is *The Body Ecology Diet* by Donna Gates which teaches how to control yeast and to restore the inner "ecosystem" by using food-combining and good nutrition.

Grapefruit seed extract, acidophilus, garlic and Pau d'Arco (also known as Taheebo) are all extremely beneficial supplements used to control yeast.

Hypoglycemia (Low Blood Sugar)

Ever get that afternoon lull where a nap just sounds so good? Think about what you ate up to that point… a high intake of refined carbohydrates will cause a sudden rise in blood sugar. To counteract this, insulin is produced. As the blood sugar drops, hormones like glucagon, cortisol and adrenaline are produced to bring the sugar level back to normal. The resulting symptoms that can occur are fatigue, light-headedness, irritability and depression. This drop in blood sugar also produces a craving for food, especially foods that will help raise the sugar levels again. Some people call this resulting cycle the crab cycle because when the blood sugar drops watch out, people get crabby!

Now think of those poor kids who are given cereals with lots of milk and sugar for breakfast, or worse yet, donuts! At lunch they eat more refined carbohydrates followed by a candy bar, all the while guzzling down a sugar-packed soda. No wonder they can't concentrate! The best thing to do to avoid sudden blood sugar crashes is to eat several small meals a day that are higher in complex carbohydrates and protein. Adding essential fatty acids to smoothies helps to slow down the processing of the fruit sugars (see *Orange Sunrise* recipe in the Breakfasts & Beverages section). Avoid refined carbohydrates, caffeine and other unwholesome foods.

Foods that I have found to be very helpful and easy to cart around during the day are hard-boiled eggs, grapefruit, avocados, a small amount of dried apricots and almonds. Chromium Picolinate, vitamins E, C and B-complex are important supplements. Last but certainly my favorite, spirulina (I like carob mint flavored tablets or powder made by Organic By Nature).

Before we head to the recipe section, there is one last piece of information that I think is important to consider. We live in a culture that indoctrinates us to believe that we need to eat massive amounts of protein to survive. What we believe has a great impact on what we do. A lot of erroneous beliefs have been embedded in our thinking. Guess who told us all about the need for meat and dairy? That propaganda, paid for by the meat and dairy industries, got us all to believe that we couldn't be healthy without those foods. More money to be made!

All that information about milk providing us with bone-building calcium whipped up lots of increased dairy consumption. Consider this: calcium is found in almonds, fruits, vegetables, beans and grains. Animal products are a form of dense protein requiring large amounts of calcium to process them. This actually robs the body of calcium. It is more probable that as a nation we suffer more from protein excess than deficiency. Think about it. What are the symptoms of protein deficiency? Who do you know who has that? When we get too much protein from animal products we see all kinds of diseases, especially heart-related. Statistics for vegans vs. meat eaters speak loud and clear when it comes to heart disease.

Lastly, have you ever poured cola over a baby tooth or a ten penny nail and then gone back in a few days? If so, then you know that the cola acts as a dissolving agent. Just think about what that does to bones! Talk about robbing calcium out of your body, cola makes animal consumption look tame!

Eating Vegetables Worked for Daniel!

Daniel 1:3-20: Then the king ordered Ashpenaz, chief of his court officials, to bring in some of the Israelites from the royal family and the nobility—young men without any physical defect, handsome, showing aptitude for every kind of learning, well informed, quick to understand and qualified to serve in the king's palace. He was to teach them the language and literature of the Babylonians. The king assigned them a daily amount of food and wine from the king's table. They were to be trained for three years, and after that they were to enter the king's service. Among these were some from Judah; Daniel, Hananiah, Mishael and Azariah.

The chief official gave them new names: to Daniel, the name Belteshazzar; to Hananiah, Shadrach; to Mishael, Meshach; and to Azariah, Abednego.

But Daniel resolved not to defile himself with the royal food and wine, and he asked the chief official for permission not to defile himself this way.

Now God had caused the official to show favor and sympathy to Daniel, but the official told Daniel, "I am afraid of my lord the king, who has assigned your food and drink. Why should he see you looking worse than the other young men your age? The king would then have my head because of you."

Daniel then said to the guard, whom the chief official had appointed over Daniel, Hananiah, Mishael and Azariah, "Please test your servants for ten days. Give us nothing but vegetables to eat and water to drink. Then compare our appearance with that of the young men who eat the royal food, and treat your servants in accordance with what you see."

So he agreed to this and tested them for ten days.

At the end of the ten days they looked healthier and better nourished than any of the young men who ate the royal food. So the guard took away their choice food and the wine they were to drink and gave them vegetables instead. To these four young men God gave knowledge and understanding of all kinds of literature and learning. And Daniel could understand visions and dreams of all kinds.

At the end of the time set by the king to bring them in, the chief official presented them to Nebuchadnezzar. The king talked with them, and he found none equal to Daniel, Hananiah, Mishael and Azariah; so they entered the king's service.

In every matter of wisdom and understanding about which the king questioned them, he found them ten times better than all the magicians and enchanters in his whole kingdom.

RawSome Recipes

Created by Robyn Boyd

How to Best Use the Recipe Section

Each recipe section is divided into two parts:

1. **RAW:** recipes whose ingredients are all raw (presented ahead of the "SOME" recipes) and have this icon. *R*

2. **SOME:** recipes containing some ingredients that are cooked and display this icon. *S*

*R*ecipes that have been tried and approved by "kid palates" receive the **"RawSome Kid Recipe!"** seal of approval. Of course, not all kids like the same tastes and textures, so experiment with your children and see how these recipes might be converted into ones they would enjoy.

If you are transitioning to a healthier lifestyle, a great way to approach this is to upgrade old favorites with healthier choices from the SOME section. A nice goal is to keep adding in new recipes each week. In addition, gradually shift the balance of cooked to raw food over to a 75% RAW to 25% SOME cooked ratio.

Some people like to mix raw foods with some cooked at every meal. With this approach the plate can be divided into fourths ($3/4$ raw, $1/4$ cooked) making it easy to see how much raw to put on the plate versus cooked.

Other people prefer to eat all raw until dinnertime, where some cooked food is added to a mostly raw meal. Each person has to find what works best to make a healthier eating lifestyle do-able and not something that is either too extreme or too consuming.

Breakfasts & Beverages

(Recipes in this section are all raw except Amé Wineless Coolers)

Photo: Porridge & Papaya Pudding (page 56)

Good Morning Granola! R

RawSome Kid Recipe!

NOTE: dehydrator needed

(My version of an original recipe created by Rose Lee Calabro)

> **2 cups almonds, soaked 12 hours in a separate bowl**
> **½ cup each: pumpkin seeds, sunflower seeds, pecans and walnuts all soaked 4 hours**
> **(soak the seeds in one bowl and the nuts in another)**
> **2 cups apples**
> **1 T. cinnamon**
> **1 T. vanilla**
> **1 tsp. salt**
> **½ cup shredded dried coconut**
> **2 or 3 pieces of dried mangos cut up into tiny pieces added after all other ingredients**
> **have been dehydrated (or substitute with ½ cup raisins or cut up dried apricots)**

1. Rinse and drain all nuts and seeds.

2. With the "S" blade of a processor, begin chunking down the almonds into small bits. Empty contents into a big mixing bowl.

3. Repeat processing with the pumpkin and sunflower seeds until all are small chunky bits, not over-processing. Add to almonds and repeat process with remaining nuts.

4. Next core and cut apples into quarters. Put through processor using the shredding device.

5. Mix all ingredients together except for the coconut and dried fruit.

6. Using a teflex sheet, spread the granola onto tray, making sure not to mound it. Dehydrate up to 24 hours at 105° until the granola is crisp and crunchy.

7. Mix the dried granola in with the coconut and dried fruit and store in a tall Mason jar for maximum shelf life. If your granola seems stale or damp as time goes on you can try re-dehydrating it, which generally perks it right up again!

Notes:

Great with **Fresh Almond Milk!** (See recipe this section.) Slightly warm the milk on cold mornings.

Without milk, this makes a great kid snack and it travels well in school lunches in baggies.

Using this same granola you can make a delicious dessert or after-school snack. Turn this granola into a parfait and serve in fancy glasses. Kids love it! See *Granola Parfaits* in *RawSome Treats* section for easy directions.

Porridge & Papaya Pudding ℞

RawSome Kid Recipe!

> 1 cup soaked and drained organic oat groats or whole oats
> 2–3 pitted dates at room temperature
> ½ tsp. cinnamon
> *Almond Milk** (approx. ¼ cup)
> 1 papaya, skinned, seeded and cut in pieces
> 1 heaping T. raw organic almond butter
> approx. 1 T. slivered almonds
> mixed berries

1. Soak one cup per serving of raw oat groats or oats in enough water to cover, overnight.

2. In the morning, drain and place in food processor with cinnamon, dates and almond milk processing until desired texture (usually quite quickly). Pour into a wide bowl.

3. Wash out processing bowl and add papaya and almond butter. Process until creamy.

4. Top the oatmeal with a heaping tablespoon or two of the blended papaya in the center of the bowl. See note below.

5. Sprinkle the slivered almonds over the oatmeal. Using an alternating pattern, place **sliced strawberries** and either **blueberries** or **blackberries** around the outside border of the bowl. Crown the papaya pudding with two sliced strawberries! Enjoy!

See photo of recipe on first page of this section

Note:
Reserve the remaining papaya blend in a covered container. Later, as a snack or dessert, blend the papaya and almond butter with a half banana for a delicious pudding.

Apple-A-Day Porridge ℞

> 1 cup steel cut oats soaked overnight
> ¼ cup buckwheat groats soaked overnight
> 2–3 pitted dates at room temperature
> 1 apple, cored and sliced
> ½ tsp. cinnamon
> *Almond Milk** **(start with about ⅛ cup and use up to ¼ cup)**

1. Soak oats and groats overnight. Rinse and drain oats and groats.

2. Process all ingredients except the apple using the "S" blade.

3. Add the apple and use the pulse setting so apple blends nicely.

*For *Fresh Almond Milk,* see recipe this section.

New Natives Breakfast Jump Start ℞

(Inspired by Sandra Ward)

> 1 cup sunflower seeds
> 2 T. flaxseeds
> 1/3 cup pumpkin seeds
> 6 dried apricots
> 1/4 cup raisins
> 1 tsp. cinnamon
> 1 1/2 cups apple juice
> 1/2 –1 banana
> 2 cups *Almond Milk** (can use rice, oat or grain milk)

Make it easy by doing the first two steps before going to bed:

1. Soak apricots, raisins and cinnamon in apple juice overnight.

2. In a separate jar, soak sunflower, flax and pumpkin seeds in water. Drain and rinse after one hour. Let sprout overnight.

3. In the morning, blend seed mixture with the apricots and apple juice until smooth and creamy.

4. Next add the banana and your choice of milk.

This drink is power-packed with taste and great nutrition for kids.

Flaxseeds—can help improve kidney function, reduce heart disease risk, and help fight cancer. Flaxseeds are high in a steroid compound known as lignans. A researcher at Toronto University named Dr. Lillian Thompson has published studies indicating lignans to be powerful anti-cancer agents particularly against colon and breast cancer. Her studies with animals have shown breast cancer reduction by 50% using flax. High in fiber and omega 3 fatty acids, flaxseeds also seem to lower levels of LDL cholesterol, the kind associated with heart disease.

Apricots—contain beta-carotene (good for the eyes) and lycopene, both shown to keep LDL cholesterol from turning rancid in the bloodstream, thereby preventing it from sticking to artery walls. Good form of fiber.

Raisins—great source of potassium, which helps to lower high blood pressure. Great source of iron for vegetarians. Iron is essential for creating hemoglobin in red blood cells, which are used by the body to transport oxygen.

Note: Never buy sulfured dried fruits, including golden raisins!

*For *Fresh Almond Milk*, see recipe this section.

Robyn's Morning Meal R

Upon arising I have 1 tsp. of **barley powder** in eight ounces of water. Anywhere from half an hour to an hour later I make the following smoothie:

> 8–10 oz. *Almond Milk**
> 2 tsps. Twinlab's Yeast Plus (brewers yeast)
> ¼ cup flaxseeds
> ½ banana
> 1 heaping tsp. Carob Mint Spirulina (made by Organic by Nature)

1. Grind flaxseeds in grinder.

2. Mix all ingredients in a blender. This smoothie fills me with wonderful nutrition and takes me all the way through a very active morning until lunchtime. (See benefits of flaxseeds under *New Natives Breakfast Jump Start* recipe).

Orange Sunrise Smoothie R

RawSome Kid Recipe!

> frozen mixed berries
> 3 oranges
> 1 tsp. Udo's Oil or Supreme 7 Oil Blend
> one frozen banana

Freeze an assortment of berries. Freeze bananas, skinless and broken into small pieces.

1. Squeeze the juice of three oranges (or if you must, buy fresh organic OJ already made).

2. Scoop out two generous portions of berries into blender. Add one large frozen banana and the fresh OJ. Add Udo's Oil or Supreme 7 Blend (1 tsp. for kids or 1 T. for adults).

   Blend and pour into a tall glass. You can slice a **strawberry** almost in half and place on the lip of the glass as a nice finishing touch.

*For *Fresh Almond Milk*, see recipe next page.

Fresh Almond Milk R

1½ cups organic almonds
4 cups purified water (or instead use 4 cups fresh coconut water
    from two coconuts for delicious coconut almond milk)
2–4 pitted dates
1 tsp. vanilla
1 tsp. cinnamon
fine mesh strainer *

1. Soak almonds in water overnight. Pit the dates and soak overnight, saving the date soak water to use later.

2. Be sure to drain and then rinse the almonds well.

    All nuts and seeds contain growth inhibitors that prevent them from sprouting prematurely if they are exposed to moisture. Some people call these growth inhibitors toxins that need to be removed, and they also recommend the skins be removed as well. If you are a purist, by all means remove the skins of the almonds! Removing the skins also makes for whiter milk. Most of the time I leave the skins on.

3. Put drained almonds in blender with the fresh coconut or purified water.

4. Add 1 tsp. cinnamon, or more depending on your taste, and 1 tsp. vanilla.

5. Add soaked dates plus soaking water. Blend and pour through fine mesh strainer.* Yum yum!

Option:

RawSome Kid Recipe!

Add approx **4 T. carob powder.** Warm and serve instead of hot chocolate. Kids love it, especially the froth from blending it in the blender once it is warmed up. Great topped off with a little sprinkle of nutmeg!

Or try adding a **frozen banana or two** to make a thick carob milk shake! By including 1 tsp. of **Organic by Nature's Carob Mint Spirulina** you add wonderful protein and a range of valuable nutrients.

* I have found that using a fine nylon mesh strainer, used by painters to strain a one-gallon bucket of paint, is ideal for this application. One kind I use is made by Intex and sold at paint stores. After pouring the almond milk in the strainer bag, use a rubber band to hold top closed. Holding the bag over a bowl, squeeze the liquid through the mesh. This sure beats milking a cow! Kids love to do this step! You can also contact Elaina Love to purchase a wonderful bag made just for this purpose, called the Amazing Nut Milk Juice and Sprout Bag. You can find this and other great info on her web site **www.purejoylivingfoods.com** or **raw4life@yahoo.com**

Yumlishious Almond Protein Drink ℞

8 oz *Almond Milk** (can also use rice or oat milk)
2 T. almond butter
1 T. brewer's yeast**
1 fresh or frozen banana

Blend all ingredients. Using a frozen banana will create a thicker creamier shake.

Option:

Can use **tahini** instead of almond butter. Adding one heaping teaspoon of **spirulina** will give you wonderful added protein.

*For fresh *Almond Milk* see recipe this section.

**I prefer Twin Labs Yeast Plus above all other brewer's yeast products as there are enzymes included to help prevent gas and indigestion problems.

Miss Molly's Favorite Juice ℞

RawSome Kid Recipe!

2 organic apples
2 organic pears

1. Wash and slice up pears and apples.

2. Put through juicer.

3. Pour juice through a fine mesh strainer and enjoy!

Apple Juice Slushies ℞

RawSome Kid Recipe!

fresh organic apple juice
plastic drink bottle*

Use a little less than one pint of fresh organic apple juice. Fill up container and freeze overnight. Place in your child's lunch box with a straw and by afternoon—*poof*—slushies! Organic grape juice works great as well.

Note:

Rubbermaid makes the perfect containers for this! They are 1-pint plastic liquid containers with a round snap down lid that has a hole in it for drinking.

*I usually like to avoid using plastic when possible. This is an exception.

Option:

Try juicing **organic red seedless grapes** in with the fresh juiced apples for a yummy blend.

Banana Almond Milk Shake R

RawSome Kid Recipe!

Recipe for one shake

> 1½ **frozen banana**
> 1 cup *Almond Milk**
> ½ **cup vanilla goat yogurt (optional)**

1. Peel six or more very ripe bananas. Break each banana into three pieces and place in gallon zip lock bag. Freeze overnight. Now you will have a surplus of frozen bananas for future shakes. Add to the freezer bag whenever you run low or have ripe bananas to spare!

2. Add all above ingredients to blender and *voila!*

Note:

For a thicker shake add more banana or for a thinner shake add more almond milk or yogurt!

Option:

Try adding one tablespoon **tahini** or **almond butter.**

Coconut Date Shake R

> 3 **young coconuts**
> 4 **pitted medjool dates at room temperature**

1. Hack open three young coconuts.

2. Scrape out the meat of all three coconuts and place in a blender.

3. Use the coconut water from one coconut and save the water from the other two to drink at another time.

4. Also add the four dates to the blender. Whirl on highest setting until you have a nice thick shake.

Note:

See photos on back of the book on how to open a coconut. Notice that I use the rear tip of a butcher knife to create the right stroke to penetrate the outer shell.

Coconut Chai R

1. Prepare the **coconut** as if you are making the *Coconut Date Shake.*

2. Brew up a batch of **Bengal Spice Tea** made by Celestial Seasonings. Use enough tea bags to make a strong dark batch.

3. While tea steeps add **4 pitted medjool dates** to the water to sweeten the brew.

4. Place warm tea, dates and some *Coconut Date Shake* into a blender and whip until there is a nice froth on the top.

5. Pour in mugs, sprinkle a little **nutmeg** on top and enjoy on a cold winter's eve!

*For Fresh Almond Milk, see recipe this section.

Wheatgrass Cocktail R

    1 oz. fresh wheatgrass juice
    juice of one lemon
    2 apples juiced

Mix all the juices together. *Cheers!*

Coconut Barley Blast R

    water from one young coconut
    1 heaping tsp. barley powder (or your favorite green powder)

Blend the two together and enjoy the sweet treat of a coconut blast to accompany your barley powder.

One A & Three Cs Juice R

    1 apple
    3 carrots
    3 sticks of celery
    ½–1 cucumber

Wash all ingredients well, juice and blend.

Sunflower Sprouts & Apple Juice R

    3 apples washed, sliced and juiced
    handfuls of fresh sunflower sprouts

Blend the two together. Refreshing and yummy!

Mellow Melon Juice R

Wash the outside of all **melons** well as they tend to have mold and dirt on the outer skins. This way when you cut through the melon you don't drag the debris through the melon meat on your knife as you slice.

Pick **your favorite melons** and slice pieces to fit in your juicer. I prefer to juice watermelon all by itself.

watermelon Lemonade R

RawSome Kid Recipe!

You can make watermelon lemonade by making a batch of lemonade using **fresh lemons, water** and **honey** and then add this to your **juiced watermelon**. A 12-lb. watermelon yields about 5 ½ quarts of juice. Stays good in fridge for about five days.

party punch R

RawSome Kid Recipe!

This recipe requires the use of a **bundt pan** (the type used for angel cakes, round with a hole in the middle).

1. Pour two packages of **frozen mixed organic berries** (Trader Joe's stocks organic raspberry and blueberries) into bundt pan.
2. Pour a 32 oz. bottle of your favorite **juice** (I usually use Organic Hibiscus Cooler made by Santa Cruz Organic) over the frozen berries in the bundt pan. If you have a really large punch bowl, it may require two bottles of juice.
3. Place the pan in the freezer overnight.
4. Fill up a punch bowl with your favorite **juice** or **lemonade** (again I use the same Hibiscus Cooler).
5. Drop the contents of the bundt pan into the punch bowl. The frozen berries and juice make a lovely floating ice to keep the punch cold. As this melts, the berries are released into the punch, making this a big hit with the kids!

Amé wineless coolers S

RawSome Kid Recipe!

This is a fabulous beverage to serve for festive occasions in place of wine!

> **2 bottles Amé Delicate White (Trader Joe's stocks it)**
> **2 kiwis**
> **enough strawberries to place one on each glass rim**
> **star fruit if available**

Amé is a delicious, gently sparkling beverage made from grape juice extract, carbonated spring water, apricot juice, citric acid and herbal extracts of limeflower, jasmine, schizandra and gentian. Pour Amé in wine glasses. Slice up kiwis and place one or two slices in each glass. Add sliced star fruit if available. Make a slit in the bottom of each strawberry and wedge on the rim of each glass. Make a toast to your health and enjoy! Amé also comes in Radiant Red and Refreshing Rosé flavors.

Coconut Almond Mango Lasse R

> 1 cup coconut almond milk (see recipe on page 59)
> 3/4 cup frozen mango chunks (Trader Joe's carries this, or just cut up a ripe
> mango into cubes and freeze overnight)

Follow directions on page 59 on how to make coconut almond milk. Process milk with mangos in blender and enjoy this delicious drink!

Coconut Almond Banana Lasse R

> 1 cup coconut almond milk (see recipe on page 59)
> 1-2 large frozen bananas

Follow directions on page 59 on how to make coconut almond milk. Process milk with bananas in blender. The more banana used the thicker and creamier.

Molly's Mango Lasse R

(Created by my daughter, Molly, age 12)

RawSome Kid Recipe!

> 1 cup organic orange juice
> ½ ripe banana
> 8–10 pieces frozen mango chunks (Trader Joe's carries this, or just cut up a ripe
> mango into cubes and freeze overnight)
> ¾ cup vanilla goat yogurt (for vegans use almond milk)
> 1 ice cube

Blend on high until you have a thick, creamy lasse. Great afternoon snack on a warm day!

Yumlíshíous Lunchtíme Items!

Raw

Some

Photo: Sandra's Brilliantly Beyond Tuna Salad (page 69)

what to Pack in the School Lunch Box?

1. Carrot sticks with *Mock Ranch Dressing (pg.77)*
2. Celery with almond butter and raisins
3. *Almond Joy Balls (pg.148)*
4. Almonds and raisins
5. Pistachio nuts
6. Bonobo's Coconut Date Macaroons *(pg.148)*
7. Fruit salad
8. *Apple Slushie (pg. 60)*
9. Fruit roll ups
10. *Gorgeous Guacamole (pg. 132)* and veggie chips
11. Assorted dried fruit
12 Macadamia nuts
13. Carrot raisin salad
14. *Yum Yum Yam salad (pg. 90)*/potato salad
15. Avocado sandwiches
16. Almond butter and banana sandwich
17. Stuffed pita pockets
18. *Cool Cucumber Salad (pg. 70)*
19. Pasta salad
20. Kiwis, grapes, orange slices
21. Rice cakes with almond butter
22. Rice cakes with hummus
23. Assorted dehydrated fruits and veggies
24. Broccoli salad *(pgs. 84 & 85)*
25. *Santa Cruz Solar Tacos (pg. 68)*
26. *Sandra's Brilliantly Beyond Tuna* sandwiches *(pg. 69)*
27. *It's A Wrap* sandwiches *(pg. 70)*

Santa Cruz Solar Tacos

RawSome Kid Recipe!

Begin with a batch of *Cashew Paté* mix:

> **1 cup cashews**
> **1 cup sunflower seeds**
> **8 oz. fresh salsa or 1 jar of your favorite organic salsa**
> **corn tortillas**
> **diced ripe tomatoes**
> **diced avocado**
> **sunflower seed sprouts**
> **diced red onion**

1. Place cashews and sunflower seeds in processor. Grind to a fine meal.

2. Slowly add salsa until the consistency is moist but stiff enough to spread as paté.

3. Hold tortilla in your hand taco-style and fill with paté mix. Top with tomatoes, avocado and sprouts. Eat on the spot or wrap up and send this off with the kids for school lunches. Great for picnics.

See photo of recipe on front cover of this book.

Sandra's Brilliantly Beyond Tuna Salad R

(Inspired by New Natives Workshop)

> **1 cup each sunflower seeds and almonds, soaked**
> **1/4 cup brown sesame seeds, soaked**
> **1/2 cup celery, chopped very fine**
> **1/2 cup fresh parsley, finely snipped**
> **1/3 cup purified water**
> **1/4 cup fresh lemon juice**
> **1 tsp. onion powder**
> **1 tsp. kelp granules**
> **1 tsp. garlic powder**
> **Vegenaise**

1. Soak nuts and seeds for three hours and let drain and sprout for eight hours (or overnight).

2. Blend nuts, seeds and seasonings in a food processor.

3. Add veggies, water, and lemon juice and mix well.

4. Continue mixing in the processor and use enough Vegenaise to blend as if tuna. It is best to chill before serving.

Helpful hints:
Scoop on lettuce and surround with **tomatoes**, or stuff into **celery** or **mushrooms**.
Roll up in **lettuce leaves** with **sprouts** to make delicious finger food.

Option:
Substitute **lime** for lemon and **cilantro** for parsley. You can also add finely chopped **red bell peppers** and mix in with nut-seed blend.

See photo of recipe on first page of this section.

It's A Wrap!   R

> 6 sundried tomatoes
> 3 large fresh tomatoes
> 1 clove garlic
> 1–2 figs
> 1 cup spinach leaves
> 1 avocado diced
> 1 cup grated carrots
> Wraps—find your favorite kind. If you are not allergic to wheat,
> the healthiest is a sprouted whole wheat tortilla. I have seen cilantro,
> spinach and tomato basil wraps that are great for a more festive look!

1. Soak sundried tomatoes in warm water for half an hour, then drain.
2. Place in processor with tomatoes.
3. Add garlic.
4. Now add figs.
5. Spread the tomato fig sauce on wrap.
6. Fill with fresh spinach leaves, avocados and grated carrots!

It's A Wrap!

Cool Cucumber Salad   R

RawSome Kid Recipe!

> 1 organic English cucumber (the long thin kind often grown in hothouses)

Mix:

> ⅓ cup brown rice vinegar
> 1 tsp. honey or agave
> ½ red onion diced fine
> **Gamazio to taste** (See *Honorable Hors d'Oeuvres…*)

1. Dice or slice cucumber however you like. To get the most nutrients, you may leave
   outer skin on if you wash thoroughly. For a whiter-looking salad, remove skin.
2. Combine the rest of the ingredients, toss with cucumbers, and serve on the side with wraps!

Ginger Garlic Tabbouleh! ℜ

2 cups finely ground bulgur wheat (found in bulk bins)
2–3 T. rice vinegar
1 heaping tsp. fresh grated ginger
1–2 cloves minced garlic
2 T. olive oil
1–2 tsp. raw honey or agave
5 scallions finely chopped
½ cup chopped fresh parsley
½ cup chopped fresh cilantro
1 cup grated carrots
Celtic Sea Salt to taste

1. Place bulgur in a medium bowl and cover with water. Allow to soak for 30 minutes or until soft. Drain through a colander.

2. Meanwhile, in a medium bowl, combine vinegar, oil ginger, garlic, honey and salt.

3. Whisk until blended. Taste and then adjust with honey and more oil if too vinegary.

4. When the bulgur is good and soft, add the parsley, cilantro and carrots and toss with the dressing.

Option:
To make this even more nutritious, try adding ½ cup **sprouted quinoa** (soak for two hours then let sprout all day) and ¼ – ½ cup **chopped fresh mint.**

Serving Suggestions:
Use **chopped tomatoes** to form a decorative ring. Serve in a salad bowl and dot tomatoes on top or stuff inside **pita pockets.** This is a great lunch dish!

Avocado Boats ℞

> ½ cup sunflower seeds
> ½ cup almonds
> 1 large stalk celery
> ½ of a red bell pepper
> 1 small tomato
> ¼ of a red onion
> 1 clove garlic minced fine
> Celtic Sea Salt to taste

Paté

1. Soak sunflower seeds and almonds overnight and drain.
2. Dice up small: celery, red bell pepper, tomato and onion.
3. Mix everything together in a food processor and add garlic and salt.
4. Slice avocado in half and stuff with paté!

Avocado Nori Wrap Sandwich ℞

> 1 sheet nori
> 1 avocado, mashed
> 1 tsp. lemon juice
> 1 carrot grated
> sunflower seed sprouts
> salt-free Spike or kelp granules

Mix avocado with lemon and seasoning. Spread evenly on nori sheet. Sprinkle with grated carrots and sprouts, wrap up, and you have a quick and nutritious lunch!

Open Face Manna Sandwich S

RawSome Kid Recipe!

> Manna bread (sprouted raw grain bread found in most health foods stores
>   and kept in fridge)
> raw almond butter
> honey
> sliced bananas

Spread bread with a generous amount of almond butter. Add a thin layer of honey, and top with fresh sliced bananas.

Veggie Burger & Homemade Fries! §

RawSome Kid Recipe!

Amy's Organic California veggie burgers
Alvarado Bakery's sprouted wheat buns (Trader Joe's has these)
Grapeseed Oil Vegenaise
organic pickles
lettuce and tomatoes
1 large onion, sliced
5 shiitake mushrooms, sliced
2 T. organic butter (Trader Joe's carries this at a great price!)
assortment of your favorite potatoes
2–3 T. organic olive oil

1. Prepare burgers as directed on package.
2. Sauté sliced onions and shiitake mushrooms in butter to smother on top of burgers!
3. Slice up an assortment of your favorite potatoes into any shapes you want.
4. Place in zip lock gallon size bag and sprinkle in **garlic salt** and **Celtic Sea Salt.**
5. Pour in olive oil to coat. Zip up and shake all around.
6. Disperse on a baking pan or cookie sheet. Bake at 400° until crisp and brown.
7. Check often and turn over once the first side looks golden.

Option:
You can also use the *Lovely Lentil, Millet & Nut Loaf* recipe (see *Dinner Delights* section), formed into patties, for burgers.

Salads & Salad Dressings

Raw

Some

Home Base Sauce & House Dressing R

> 1 cup organic olive oil
> juice of 2 lemons (Meyers lemons are the best)
> 6–8 cloves garlic minced
> 2 T. fruit juice sweetened apricot jam
> 1 tsp. cumin
> 1 tsp. Italian seasoning
> Celtic Sea Salt

Place all ingredients in a Mason jar, making sure lid is tight, and shake vigorously.

Mock Ranch R

RawSome Kid Recipe!

> ¼ cup almonds, soaked overnight
> 3 T. Udo's Oil or Pacific Hemp Supreme 7 Oil Blend
> juice of 1 lemon
> 2 cloves of garlic, minced
> ½ –1 cup Grapeseed Oil Vegenaise
> touch of honey
> ¼ to ½ tsp. kelp granules (to taste)

1. Drain and rinse the almonds.
2. Blanch the almonds by pouring boiling water into a bowl. Add almonds for thirty seconds and slowly add cold water until the water is warm not hot. Now just use your index finger and thumb to pop the skins off.
3. Add the blanched almonds to all the other ingredients and thoroughly blend them in a food processor. This yields a nice thick dip, great with fresh cut-up **peppers, cucumbers, celery, carrots, broccoli** and **cauliflower.**

Honey Mustard a la Udo's R

> 2 T. Udo's Oil
> juice of 1 lemon
> 1–2 tsp. stone ground salt-free mustard (Westbrae makes a nice one)
> 1 tsp. raw honey

Mix all ingredients in processor or blender. Adjust to taste by adding more honey.

Blend together all ingredients for each dressing on this page in a blender or food processor unless otherwise specified.

Creamy Feta Dressing R

    1 cup *Home Base Dressing* (see recipe in this section)
    1 heaping T. Vegenaise
    1 chunk of organic feta cheese (Trader Joe's makes a nice one)
    water if needed to thin the dressing

Poppy Seed Lime Salad Dressing R

    juice of 1 or 2 limes
    1/3 cup Udo's Oil or olive oil
    1 tsp. poppy seeds
    1 tsp. honey or 1–2 pitted medjool dates
    Celtic Sea Salt to taste

1. Blend all ingredients in blender except poppy seeds.

2. Add poppy seeds and blend on low, only to mix in.

Cucumber Yogurt Dressing R

    1 cup plain goat yogurt
    1/2 large cucumber
    1–2 cloves garlic
    1 tsp. kelp
    1 tsp. honey

Red Bell Pepper & Almond Dressing R

    1 cup almonds, soaked overnight then rinsed and drained
    1 red bell pepper
    1 cup purified water
    1 or 2 garlic cloves
    1 tsp. nutritional yeast
    1/2 tsp. kelp
    2 pitted dates

Mix all ingredients in blender. Dressing thickens up in time, so add more water if necessary.

Option:
Add **Udo's Oil** or **Pacific Hemp Supreme 7 Oil Blend** if you need your daily dose of essential fatty acids.

Blend together all ingredients for each dressing on this page in a blender or food processor unless otherwise specified.

Almond Delight Salad Dressing ℞

> ½ cup almonds soaked overnight (Blanched gives you a whiter dressing. See
>   *Mock Ranch* for how to blanch.)
> ½ cup organic olive oil
> ¾ cup purified water
> 2 T. onion flakes
> ¼ tsp. Celtic Sea Salt
> 2 pitted medjool dates
> juice of 1 lemon
> 1 large clove garlic

Sweet Summer Slaw with Almond Mayo ℞

Almond Mayo:

> 1 cup soaked almonds
> 1 fresh lemon juiced
> 1 T. agar agar
> 2 tsp. onion flakes
> ¾ cup water
> 3 soaked dates, pitted
> ¼ tsp. salt
> ½ cup olive oil

1. Blend all ingredients above and chill for several hours.

Slaw:

> 1 head green cabbage shredded
> 1 red apple diced
> ½ cup celery
> ½ cup currants
> 2–3 carrots grated
> 1 tsp. dill
> Celtic Sea Salt to taste
> slivered almonds (optional)

2. Mix together all slaw ingredients above in a salad bowl.

3. Add chilled *Almond Mayo* and toss well.

Red Head Dressing R

⅓ cup olive oil
2 ripe tomatoes
½ red bell pepper
1 T. brown rice vinegar
1 tsp. apricot jam or 1–2 pitted dates
1–2 cloves garlic

Blend together all ingredients. Great served on **red leaf lettuce!**

Sweet Curry Dressing I R

1–2 pitted medjool dates, soaked
¾–1 tsp. curry powder
½ cup Vegenaise
¾ cup *Almond Milk* (see *Breakfasts & Beverages*)
1 T. Udo's Oil

Sweet Curry Dressing II R

4 T. olive oil
2 T. fresh lemon juice
2 cloves garlic
1 tsp. curry powder
½ tsp. cumin
½ tsp. powdered ginger or 1 tsp. fresh ginger
4 pitted dates, soaked
1½ tsp. Real Salt
1 tsp. honey or agave (more if you like)

Blend either dressing and toss with:

Hearts of romaine, two large diced **ripe tomatoes, cubed avocado, sunflower sprouts** and **lentil sprouts.**

Or:

Spring salad mix with edible flowers, two handfuls of **soaked almonds,** two handfuls of **cashews,** ½ cup **currants** and sliced **mushrooms**

Summer Splendor Salad R

2 ears of corn with kernels removed
1 red and 1 yellow bell pepper, diced
1/2 red onion, diced
3 stalks celery, diced
1 cucumber, diced
1 bunch of cilantro
2 ripe avocados, cubed
Home Base Dressing enough to cover (see *Salad Dressings*)

Mix all ingredients well. Season with **kelp**. Top with chopped **soaked almonds** and **sunflower sprouts**.

Yellow & Red Cherry Tom Salad R

2 ears of white sweet corn with kernels removed
2 cups of assorted sweet yellow and red cherry tomatoes
1/2 red onion, diced
1/2 cup basil, cut into small pieces
2–3 cloves garlic minced fine
1/2 cup fresh lemon juice
3 T. olive oil
kelp
Celtic Sea Salt

1. Mix garlic, lemon juice, oil, kelp and salt (to taste) in a nice serving bowl.

2. Slice tomatoes in half and then add with remaining ingredients into bowl.

3. Toss and serve on individual salad plates.

Option:
Sprinkle with **goat chevre**.

Spa Salad R

> 1 large head of butter lettuce
> 2 small apples, cut in small chunks
> fresh fennel, sliced like celery pieces
> 1 large avocado, sliced
> 1 red bell pepper, sliced in strips
> sunflower seed sprouts
> ½ cup *Honey 'N Nuts Munchie Mix* (see *Honorable Hors d'Oeuvres…*)

1. Toss lettuce, apples, and fennel in a large serving bowl or platter with **Home Base Dressing** (see *Salad Dressings*).

2. Fan out the avocado slices into a circle on top, in the center of the salad.

3. Make a circle of sprouts around the lower edges of the avocado circle and also clump a bunch in the very middle of the bowl, being the center of the avocado circle.

4. Sprinkle the nut mixture to top the salad.

5. Arrange sliced bell peppers around the outside edges of the bowl.

See photo of recipe on front cover of this book.

Westernized Greek Salad with capers R

> **organic feta cheese** (for those transitioning or non-vegan it is best if you can find raw organic feta cheese otherwise vegans can substitute with pieces of raw young coconut meat)
> 1 red onion
> 3 cucumbers
> 12 Kalamata olives, diced
> ½ jar of capers
> 4 cloves of garlic, minced
> 8 plump juicy ripe tomatoes
> 1 large avocado, diced
> Celtic Sea Salt to taste
> Tony's Italian Seasoning

Mix all the ingredients together and chill!

Greener Than Green Salad R

2 cups Romaine, broken in pieces
1/2 cup buckwheat greens
1/2 cup sunflower sprouts
3 green onions
1/4 cup celery, chopped
2 T. chopped parsley
1/2 bunch of fresh basil washed and de-stemmed
1 ripe avocado
1/2 cucumber sliced

1. Combine all ingredients.
2. Add salad dressing of your choice.
3. Toss and serve on individual salad plates.

Option:

Get creative! Add anything you like that is green to this salad.

Perfect to serve on St. Patrick's Day! This is a great way to make it fun for kids to enjoy green salads. Have them help you figure out how to make a special all-green salad using their choice of green ingredients. You could make a green salad dressing out of **avocados.** Have them draw little leprechauns or four leaf clovers that they cut out and place by each salad plate. Enjoy and most of all make it fun!

Purple & Red Confetti Salad R

1 large head of romaine lettuce
1 red onion, diced
4 celery stalks, diced small
1 red beet, shredded in food processor
1 purple potato, shredded in processor
4 ripe tomatoes, diced
1/2 cup sunflower seeds
1/2 small purple cabbage

1. Toss all ingredients with **Honey Mustard a la Udo's Dressing.**
2. Serve on large dinner plates. Use a paper towel to wipe the rim of the plate clean.
3. Turn 1/2 of a purple cabbage into confetti with "S" blade of processor.
4. Sprinkle the purple confetti cabbage around the outside rim of the plate for a festive touch.

Corn Salad R

    fresh corn off two large cobs
    1/2 **red onion or 3 scallions**, diced (depending on your preference)
    3/4 **cup red, orange, and yellow bell peppers**, diced
    1 **avocado**, diced

Option:
Add fresh diced **mild green chilies**.

Dressing:

    juice of one lemon
    juice of one lime
    1 to 2 cloves fresh garlic, minced
    1/2 **bunch of cilantro**, finely chopped
    honey or agave to taste

Mix all ingredients and toss with dressing.

Broccoli & Cranberry Salad R

RawSome Kid Recipe!
1 **large bunch of broccoli**, broken up into bite-size bits
3/4 **cup dried cranberries**, sweetened in apple juice*
1/2– 1 **cup Vegenaise mayo**
3/4 **cup cashews**
red onion, diced (optional)

Place all ingredients in a festive salad bowl.

Kids actually love this salad! Great for the holidays, too.

Note:
Some health food stores sell dried cranberries that have already been sweetened with apple juice. If you can't find this, then you might try doing it yourself instead of getting dried cranberries that have been sweetened with sugar.

Broccoli & Friends Salad R

RawSome Kid Recipe!

> 1 bunch broccoli
> 1 head cauliflower
> 1 bunch of scallions
> 2 diced red peppers

Chop up veggies and toss with **Mock Ranch Dressing** (see *Salad Dressings*).

Popeye's Special Spinach Salad R
with Honey Mustard Dressing

> 2–4 cups tender young fresh spinach
> 4 or 5 ripe tomatoes, diced
> 1/2 red onion, diced
> 1/2–1 cup red kidney beans (optional)
> diced avocado

Assemble and toss with **Honey Mustard Dressing a la Udo's** (see *Salad Dressings*).

Non Vegan Option:
Add two to four **hard boiled eggs** (depending on how big your salad is and how many you are feeding) plus **crumbled organic goat feta cheese** (Trader Joe's carries a great one).

Spinach Salad with Cashews & Shiitakes R

> fresh young spinach leaves, rinsed and drained
> 3/4 cup organic cashews
> orange cherry tomatoes
> shiitake mushrooms, sliced
> 1/2 red onion, diced

Toss salad with **Almond Bell Pepper Dressing** (see *Salad Dressings*).

Option:
Sauté **onions** and **shiitake mushrooms** in **Home Base Dressing** (see *Salad Dressings*) and pour warm over the spinach. Add **cashews** and **tomatoes**. Toss with dressing.

Marinated Green Beans & Walnuts ℞
in Apricot Dressing

> 1 lb. green beans
> ½ cup chopped fresh basil
> 1 small red onion, diced
> 2 stalks celery, diced fine
> cherry tomatoes, sliced in half
> fresh corn off the cob
> ¾ cup chopped walnuts

Marinate in **Home Base Sauce** (see *Salad Dressings*) but add one additional heaping tsp. of apricot jam.

Asian Pear Salad with Mint Dressing ℞

> 1 head romaine lettuce
> 1 ripe avocado, diced
> 1–2 Asian pears, diced
> ¼ small red onion, diced fine
> handful of mixed nuts or *Honey 'n Nuts Munchie Mix* recipe (see *Honorable Hors d'Oeuvres…*)

Dressing:

> ¾ cup Vegenaise
> juice of 1 small lemon
> 1 clove garlic
> 2 T. Udo's Oil or flax oil
> 1 small bunch of fresh mint
> 1 T. honey or agave

Arrange salad in bowl using all the ingredients. Toss with dressing and serve.

Store leftover dressing in a glass jar with a lid in fridge for about three days.

Notes:
This dressing is delicious as "secret sauce" on sandwiches.

Great when used in **pita pockets** filled with fresh **cucumbers**, **tomatoes** and **sprouts**.

Simple Salad for One R

> 1½ T. fresh lemon juice
> 1½ T. organic virgin olive oil
> salt to taste
> 1 clove garlic, minced
> ½ tsp. agave or honey

1. Start with a medium size stainless steel bowl. Place all ingredients in the bottom of the bowl and stir vigorously, making sure the honey or agave mixes in well.

2. Now add favorite ingredients. It can be as simple as **lettuce** and **tomatoes.** I like to do lettuce, fresh chopped tomatoes, diced **sweet red onions, grated carrots, cucumbers** and **celery.**

3. Toss well and eat right out of the bowl!

East West Mix Salad Supreme R

> 1 small green cabbage, shredded fine
> 1 head romaine, washed and cut up
> fresh (or frozen) peas
> 1 bunch scallions, diced
> chopped fresh cilantro
> slivered almonds

Mix salad and toss with the following dressing:

> ⅓ cup olive oil (or blend with sesame oil)
> juice of ½ large, fresh orange or tangerine
> approx. 1 T. brown rice vinegar
> 1 tsp. honey
> 1 T. black sesame seeds

Poppy Seed Coleslaw R

> purple and green cabbage, cut up for slaw
> 2 large carrots, grated

Mix with:

> 1 cup Grapeseed Oil Vegenaise
> 1 or 2 cloves garlic
> 1 or 2 tsp. apricot jam
> 1 tsp. poppy seeds

Sesame Seaweed Salad R

1 cup arame
1 cup hijiki
4 mushrooms, sliced
1 T. sesame seeds
1/4 cup brown rice vinegar
1 T. sesame oil or olive oil
1 tsp. raw honey
fresh grated ginger to taste

1. Soak the arame in filtered water for 15 minutes and drain.
2. Soak hijiki for 30 minutes, rinse and drain.
3. Slice mushrooms and mix with seaweed.
4. Mix oil, vinegar, ginger and honey.
5. Pour over seaweed.
6. Sprinkle with sesame seeds.

Option:
Try thoroughly rinsing a handful of dulse and adding to the mix or experiment with other types of seaweed.

Black & White Arame Salad R

1/2 cup arame, soaked 15 minutes
1/2 cup grated jicama
1 glove garlic, chopped fine
2 T. fresh cilantro, chopped fine
1 1/2 T. organic olive oil
1 1/2 T. lemon juice
1/2 tsp. grated ginger
salt to taste

1. First mix the lemon, oil, garlic, ginger and salt in the bottom of the serving bowl.
2. Stir in the cilantro, arame and jicama.
3. Let flavors absorb and blend. Serve at room temperature or refrigerate.

wonderful waldorf salad R

3 large red apples, cubed
4 stalks of celery, diced small
¹/₂ cup raisins or fruit juice sweetened dried cranberries
¹/₂ cup chopped walnuts

1. Place all ingredients in a large serving bowl and mix with *Almonnaise.*

2. Add more raisins, cranberries, and/ or walnuts if desired.

Option:

For a unique addition, add one cubed avocado! This can be a meal in itself and is especially good as a lunch that can be packed and carried with you. This recipe is perfect for the holiday season.

Almonnaise R

1 cup almonds, soaked overnight
1¹/₂ cups purified water
1¹/₂ tsps. onion flakes
¹/₂ tsp. Celtic Sea Salt
2 T. agar agar
5–6 pitted dates, soaked overnight
juice of two lemons
1 cup organic olive oil

1. Blend almonds and water in a food processor.

2. Next, add onion flakes, salt and agar agar while continuing to blend.

3. Add the lemon juice and the dates (making sure they are pitted). When creamy, slowly drizzle in 1 cup olive oil.

4. Mix mayo with **Waldorf** ingredients.

Yum Yum Yam Salad S

RawSome Kid Recipe!

> 6 large garnet yams
> 3/4 cup Vegenaise
> small amount of mustard (if you like)
> 1 bunch of scallions, diced
> small bunch of parsley, chopped fine
> 1/2 package of organic frozen peas
> 5 sticks celery, diced into small pieces
> *Gamazio* (see *Honorable Hors d'Oeuvres...*) or salt-free Spike

1. Steam yams until soft but still firm.
2. In a large stainless steel bowl, cut yams into chunks and mix with mayo and *Gamazio*.
3. Add all other ingredients and stir gently.
4. Place in a nice serving dish and garnish with **parsley sprigs.**
5. Store in an air-tight container in fridge and it will stay good for three days.

Note:
For non-vegans, you can slice up three or four **hard boiled eggs.**

Christmas Quinoa Salad S

> 1 cup quinoa, soaked for at least 2 hours and rinsed well
> 2 cups purified water
> 1 bunch kale
> 2 T. *Home Base Sauce* (see *Salad Dressings*)
> handful of sundried tomatoes, soaked for 2 hours
> organic feta, cut in small cubes
> handful of sunflower sprouts as garnish

1. Heat quinoa in water just to boiling, then simmer over low heat. Be sure to check on it as it cooks in about 20–30 minutes.
2. Wash kale thoroughly but leave damp.
3. Sauté kale in *Home Base Sauce* until crisp but tender.
4. Drain sundried tomatoes and cut up into little pieces.
5. Mix all ingredients together in a festive serving bowl.
6. Chill and top with sunflower sprouts.

Options:
For more raw ingredients, substitute any **raw greens** of your choice for the cooked kale.

Warm Winter Salad S

RawSome Kid Recipe!

> 2 T. *Home Base Sauce* (see *Salad Dressings*)
> 1 yellow onion, diced
> 1 cup mushrooms, sliced
> 3 hard boiled eggs
> ½ cup currants
> 1 cup shredded carrots
> spinach to fill a large salad bowl

Ginger Sesame Dressing:

> 4 T. olive and/or Udo's Oil
> 2 T. brown rice vinegar
> 1 tsp. fresh grated ginger
> 1½ T. raw honey
> 1 T. sesame seeds
> 1 clove garlic, minced
> **Celtic Sea Salt to taste**

1. Sauté onions and mushrooms in *Home Base Sauce.*

2. Fill salad bowl with spinach, carrots and currants.

3. Add the cooked warm mushrooms and onions.

4. Toss with dressing and top with warm sliced hard boiled eggs.

Festive Winter Salad S

This is one of my favorite salads for special occasions!

RawSome Kid Recipe!

> 1 head Romaine lettuce
> 1 head butter lettuce
> 1 avocado, cut in cubes
> ½ red onion, sliced
> ½ chopped pecans
> organic feta cheese, crumbled
> 2 crisp ripe pears, diced into 1-inch chunks
> *Homemade Croutons* (see *Honorable Hors d'Oeuvres...*)

Toss with **Spectrum Naturals Raspberry Omega 3 Vinaigrette Dressing**.

Note:
Technically, this is not the best food combining!

Soups & Stews

Raw

Some

Photo: Rawsome Ratatouille (page 101)

Sweet Red Pepper And Coconut Soup ℝ

(This is a fabulous soup inspired from eating at Bonobo's Restaurant, 18 E. 23rd St., New York, NY)

> **3 large red bell peppers sliced**
> **meat of three coconuts**
> **coconut water from one coconut**
> **Celtic Sea Salt to taste**

1. Slice the peppers in quarters and purée in a food processor.

2. Strain the liquid and discard the pepper meat.

3. Process pepper juice, coconut water and coconut meat with "S" blade until all are finely blended. Add salt to taste.

Tahini Lemon Swirl

> **¼ cup tahini**
> **2 T. lemon juice**
> **2 T. nama shoyu**
> **1 tsp. agave**
> **coconut water if needed to thin out the sauce**

1. Combine all ingredients and mix until smooth and the consistancy is that of a thick oil. Add coconut water if needed.

2. Using a bottle with a narrow cap (such as a mustard bottle) or an eye dropper, drizzle the swirl sauce in three lines horizontal lines across the top of the soup. Then drag four or five vertical lines through the horizontal lines with a chopstick or a knife, creating a feathering look! This makes for a festive and deliciously appetizing soup.

Option:

Use a handful of sundried tomatoes made by **Just Tomato Bits** (800-537-1985). Blend the tomatoes on high to turn them into a fine powder. Sprinkle the fine tomato powder on top of soup for a wonderful flavor burst!

Cream of Fresh Tomato Soup ℝ

> **4 large ripe tomatoes**
> **6 large leaves of fresh basil**
> **¼ small red onion**
> **½ tsp. Real Salt or Celtic Sea Salt**
> **½ large ripe avocado**

Blend all ingredients in a food processor with the "S" blade.

This is especially delicious when tomatoes are at the peak of the season.

Cool Cucumber Soup R

2 cucumbers
4 stalks celery
1/2 sweet onion
1 T. lemon juice
2 T. fresh cilantro
2 cups sunflower sprouts
Celtic Sea Salt
1 avocado

Process all ingredients in blender or food processor except for diced avocado. Pour into soup bowls and mix in chunks of avocado.

Option:
For a creamier soup process the avocado with the rest of the ingredients.

Coconut Curry Asparagus Soup R

1 bunch fresh lemongrass
1 1/2 cups water
1/2 cup fresh mint
1/2 cup sliced fresh mushrooms
Celtic Sea Salt to taste
1/2 cup slivered almonds for garnish
1/2 –1 tsp. green curry paste (made by Thai Kitchen)
contents of 2 fresh young coconuts (meat and water mixed in blender)
    or 2 cans coconut milk

1 slice fresh ginger
1/2 cup fresh cilantro chopped
4 large shiitake mushrooms, chopped
bunch of fresh asparagus
kelp granules
juice of 1 lime

1. Heat water to warm and add sliced lemongrass and ginger. Place in a jar with a lid and store in fridge overnight to allow the flavors to permeate the water. Or, for those who don't mind the enzyme-killing heat for the sake of more robust stock flavor, add sliced lemongrass and ginger to boiling water and let simmer on low for 15 minutes to bring out even more flavor.

2. Place lemongrass water in a large soup pot with coconut milk, lime juice, and curry paste. Stir well to dissolve the paste.

3. In a processor, chop up the cilantro with the mint using the "S" blade. Add these fresh herbs to the soup.

4. Cut the fresh mushrooms into thin slices and dice the shiitakes into small pieces. Stir into the soup.

5. Wash the asparagus and cut off the woody stems. Cut asparagus, starting from the top and working down, with a thin diagonal cut. Add to soup and stir all together.

6. Season to taste using Celtic Sea Salt and kelp. Garnish with slivered almonds.

7. Warm soup slightly but keep the temperature below 110 degrees to keep the enzymes alive!

Homemade Veggie Broth S

Throw in any amounts of the following, skins and all, as long as everything is thoroughly washed:

> **purple cabbage**
> **zucchini**
> **parsnips**
> **string beans**
> **celery**
> **beets**
> **potatoes**
> **2 or 3 strips kombu seaweed**
> **12 whole cloves of garlic**
> **garlic salt and Celtic Sea Salt to taste**

1. Fill stock pot half full with water. Bring water to boil first. Throw in veggies.

2. Turn down heat and let simmer about one hour. Even better when done in a crock pot.

3. Pour through a strainer and discard veggies. More than likely you will have a very pretty purple broth. Packed with potassium.

Black Bean Soup S

> **3 T. organic olive oil or organic butter**
> **1 onion, finely chopped**
> **2 cups black beans, picked over and washed**
> **8 cups veggie broth**
> **2 pieces kombu seaweed, cut into little pieces with kitchen scissors**
> **approx. ½ tsp. Celtic Sea Salt**
> **diced tomatoes and onions**
> **cilantro**
> **lime**

1. Soak beans in boiled water for several hours or overnight.

2. Sauté onion and chopped garlic in 3 T. butter or olive oil in a heavy soup pot until tender.

3. Add beans and broth plus two pieces of kombu. Bring to boil, cover and simmer two hours or until beans are tender.

4. Purée in blender or food processor in batches adding salt to taste.

5. Return puréed soup to the soup pot and reheat, stirring until the soup thickens.

6. Top with fresh chopped cilantro, some diced tomatoes and onions, and a slice of lime.

Option:
Add juice of ½ fresh lime or try sprinkling with **organic goat feta.**

Creamy Potato & White Bean Soup S

RawSome Kid Recipe!

2 medium carrots, shredded
½ cup sliced celery
4 cloves garlic, minced
1 red onion, diced
2 T. butter
4 cups organic vegetable broth
3 cups cubed potatoes
2 tsp. dried dill weed
2 cans great northern beans, rinsed and drained
1 cup plain goat yogurt
1 T. whole wheat flour
salt to taste
kelp granules

1. Melt butter in a large saucepan. Add onions, garlic, celery and carrots and sauté until tender.

2. Stir in broth, potatoes, and dill. Bring to boil and then cover and reduce to simmer until potatoes are tender, approximately 25 minutes.

3. Mash about half of the potatoes lightly with the back of spoon in the broth. Stir in the beans.

4. In a small mixing bowl, stir together the yogurt, flour, kelp granules and salt.

5. Add to potato and bean soup and cook until thickened and bubbly.

Barley Shiitake Mushroom Soup S

1 red onion, diced
2 T. olive oil or organic butter
8 cups organic vegetable broth
1 cup fresh shiitake mushrooms, sliced
3 cups lightly pearled barley, cooked
2 carrots, grated

1. Heat oil or melt butter in a large soup pot. Sauté onions and mushrooms covered for 5 minutes.

2. Add the broth, barley and seasonings to taste and simmer for about 40 minutes over low heat.

3. Stir in the grated carrots at the end and enjoy!

Adzuki Leek Soup S

(Great for nursing moms! Good way to get iron and calcium.)

> 2 cups dried adzuki beans, soaked and drained overnight
> 4 carrots, sliced
> 1 heaping T. of black strap molasses
> 3 or 4 leeks, washed and sliced
> kale or collards or both, washed and chopped
> 4 plump tomatoes, skinned and diced or can of diced organic tomatoes
> 8 cups water or veggie broth
> garlic powder and/or Celtic Sea Salt to taste

1. Boil beans in broth or water and cook for half an hour.
2. Add everything else except for collard/kale.
3. Cook until beans are tender about 30 minutes more and add greens in at the end.

Pea Soup Duet S

RawSome Kid Recipe!

> 2 cups dried split peas
> 3 cups veggie broth or filtered water
> 2 tsp. Celtic Sea Salt
> 1 tsp. cumin
> 3 stalks celery with leaves, diced
> 1 diced onion
> 4 large carrots, diced
> 3/4 bag of frozen organic peas

1. Boil **6–8 cups purified water** in a stockpot.
2. Pick through the split peas and discard anything other than the peas.
3. After water boils, turn off the heat and place the peas in the water to soak for at least two hours.
4. When you are ready to make the soup, place all ingredients in with the soaked split peas. Cover, bring to a boil, then simmer for about 1 hour until the peas are soft.
5. Purée in blender.
6. Reheat and once hot, add the frozen peas.

Using both the split peas and the frozen peas gives this soup a wonderful flavor and texture quality, hence the name: Pea Soup Duet!

Sunshine Orange Lentil Stew *S*

RawSome Kid Recipe!

> 2–3 cups lentils
> 1 large onion
> 6 cloves garlic
> 1–2 T. organic sweet cream butter
> kombu
> 2–4 pieces kale, washed and cut in small bite size pieces
> 3 large yams
> ½ cup orange juice
> 6 tomatoes, diced
> 1 tsp. curry powder
> 1 tsp. cinnamon
> 1 tsp. garlic
> *Gamazio* to taste (See *Honorable Hors d'Oeuvres…*)

1. Boil two cups water for every one cup dry lentils that you use. Turn off water, add lentils and let them soak for an hour or so with a piece of kombu.

2. Steam yams and, when soft but not mushy, remove and dice into large chunks.

3. While yams are steaming, melt butter in the bottom of a medium-sized soup pot and sauté onions and garlic in butter.

4. Add your favorite curry powder and slowly add small amounts of water so that the curry does not clump up.

5. Add lentils, diced tomatoes, spices and water into soup pot and cook over a slow heat with lid on.

6. Add orange juice and cook for approximately 20–30 minutes longer.

7. Wash and cut up kale into bite-sized pieces and add towards the end when lentils are soft.

8. Garnish with *Gamazio*.

RawSome Ratatouille S

> *Home Base Sauce* (see *Salad Dressings*)
> 1 large red onion
> 1 large eggplant, cubed (remove skin if you wish)
> 2 large zucchinis, sliced
> 2 large yellow squash zucchinis, sliced
> 2 large red bell peppers
> 1 large can of organic chopped tomatoes
> ½–3 cups broth or purified water
> handful of whole peeled cloves of garlic
> 1 tsp. garlic powder
> 1 tsp. onion powder
> 1 tsp. Italian seasoning
> *Gamazio* (see *Honorable Hors d'Oeuvres…*)
> 1 tsp. cinnamon
> 2 cans of garbanzo beans (better would be fresh home-cooked garbanzo beans, or best
>   would be sprouted garbanzo beans!)*
> avocados
> sunflower sprouts
> grated carrots

1. In a large stockpot pour enough **Home Base Sauce** to cover bottom of pot. Sauté onions until soft and translucent.

2. Add zucchinis, peppers, tomatoes, eggplant, whole cloves of garlic, seasonings and water or broth (for more of a stew add less water or broth).

3. Cook until all ingredients are soft but not mushy. Add garbanzo beans and mix all ingredients together.

4. Serve over **cooked brown rice.**

5. Top with fresh grated carrots, diced avocado, and sunflower sprouts.

Option:

*To enhance this dish with wonderful enzymes, think ahead three days. Soak one cup **dried garbanzo beans** in water for two hours. Then sprout for three full days, remembering to rinse well, 2–4 times throughout the day. Wait until Ratatouille has cooled down, so as to not destroy the valuable enzymes, and then mix in the sprouted garbanzo beans.

Another nice addition for any version of this recipe is ¾ cup of **currants**.

See photo of recipe on index page of this section.

Dinner Delights!

Raw

Some

Photo: Raw Spinach Lasagna with Cashew Ricotta (page 108)

cabbage Burritos R

In The Raw!

> ¹/₂ red onion
> 1–2 avocados
> 1 large ripe tomato
> 1 large clove garlic

1. Throw all ingredients above into food processor and blend, adding seasoning to taste.

> 1 Napa cabbage
> 2 carrots, grated
> 2 golden beets, grated
> pine nuts
> slivered almonds
> cherry tomatoes
> 1 golden beet and/or 1 red beet, shredded
> 1 carrot, shredded

2. Arrange the leaves of the cabbage around a large oval platter.

3. Spread with avocado mixture.

4. Top half of the avocado mixture with shredded carrots and the other half with shredded beets.

5. Plop a cherry tomato in the center of each burrito.

6. Sprinkle with **kelp granules** and top with pine nuts and slivered almonds.

Option:

> ¹/₂ head green cabbage, shredded
> 1 small bunch cilantro
> 1–2 ripe tomatoes, diced
> small sweet onion, diced
> juice of one lime
> salt to taste

Mix all ingredients together and put on top of avocado spread. Top with **Salsa Way Fresca** or **Mango Tango Salsa** (see *Honorable Hors d'Oeuvres…*).

Robyn's Raw Bean – os R

(Use this in place of refried beans in all your favorite Mexican recipes. Ole!)

> 2 cups almonds soaked 10-12 hours
> 1/4 macadamia nuts
> 1 cup sundried tomatoes soaked 2-4 hours
> 1 T Wholearth Spice Latin America blend (www.wholearthspice.com) or your favorite chili or Mexican spice blend
> 1 tsp. nutritional yeast flakes
> 1 tsp. garlic powder
> salt to taste

Process all ingredients in a food processor until smooth and creamy adding tomato soak water a little at a time as necessary.

Veggie Stir Unfry R

> 8 green beans, cut on the diagonal into thirds
> 6 Chinese peas, cut into thin strips
> 1 small red and 1 small orange bell pepper
> ½ head of broccoli including the stems, cut into small pieces
> 1 small bunch of baby bok choy, chopped
> a generous handful of mung bean sprouts
> 1 carrot, cut on the diagonal into thin circles, shredded or thinly sliced (your choice)
> 1 bag organic enoki white mushrooms (if available) or 6 diced shiitake mushrooms
> 1 tsp. white sesame seeds
> 1 tsp. black sesame seeds

1. Mix all ingredients together in a large serving bowl.

2. Make a batch of **Ginger Yum Yum Sauce** (see next page) and use as much or as little as your taste buds please!
    Be sure to mix everything together so the sauce coats all the ingredients.

Ginger Yum Yum Sauce ℞

(Inspired by Anna Masteller of Food in The Nude)

> **½ cup of each of the following:**
>> **fresh lemon juice**
>> **raw tahini butter**
>> **honey or agave nectar**
>> **Shoyu sauce**
> **2 cloves garlic, diced small**
> **½–1 tsp. fresh ginger, grated (or more if you love ginger!)**

Mix everything together in the blender and store in a glass jar in the fridge.

Option:
I like to add fresh **cilantro, parsley** and/or **mint** to the above ingredients. Adding the fresh green herbs makes a delicious sauce or even a wonderful salad dressing that I like to call **Green Goodness Dressing**.

Sushi Rolls with Ginger Yum Yum Dipping Sauce ℞

Filling:

> **Make a batch of** *Sandra's Brilliantly Beyond Tuna Salad*
>> **(see** *Yumlishious Lunchtime Items*)
> **carrot, red bell pepper and avocado, all cut into long thin strips**
> **sunflower sprouts, macro greens or buckwheat sprouts**
> **several sheets of nori (depending on how many rolls you want)**

1. Place a nori sheet on clean surface. With a spatula, spread approximately three tablespoons of filling on nori, starting along the edge closest to you. Make icing-like strokes to cover the sheet, leaving a half-inch border across the top uncovered.

2. In the middle of the sheet, place strips of carrots, peppers and avocados.

3. Place sprouts so they begin in the middle and stick out of one end.

4. Take the edge closest to you and place it just over the center section where the veggies are. Pull and tuck the nori back towards you, compressing the contents.

5. Now roll up all the way to the line where the filling stops.

6. Wet your fingertips and dampen the border where there is no filling, like you would to seal an envelope. Press the nori over to seal.

7. Cut rolls on the diagonal and serve with **Ginger Yum Yum Sauce** (see recipe above).

Raw Spinach Lasagna with Cashew Ricotta R

3 large zucchinis
Home Base Sauce **(see *Salad Dressings*)**

1. Begin this recipe by taking three large zucchinis and slicing them very thin lengthwise. It is best to use a mandoline for this.

2. Next marinate the zucchini "lasagna noodles" in *Home Base Sauce* to cover for 1–2 hours.

Raw Marinara Sauce

*(Also great served over **Zucchini Angel Hair Pasta**;*

see next page)

> **3 cups of blended tomatoes (romas are fine)**
> **a couple handfuls (about 2 cups) of sundried**
> **tomatoes, soaked for a couple of hours**
> **2 T. apricot jam or 2–4 pitted dates, soaked**
> **1 T. Italian seasoning**
> **fresh garlic**
> **Celtic Sea Salt to taste**
> **½ fresh sweet onion,**
> **fresh basil to taste**
> **2 T. fresh parsley**
> **a touch of olive oil**
> **2 T. capers (optional)**
> **black olives (optional)**

3. While "noodles" marinate, blend all ingredients above in processor, adding capers at the end. Set aside.

Cashew Ricotta

> 3 cups cashews (soaked for 1–2 hours)
> 2 raw bell peppers
> 1/3–1/2 cup *Home Base Sauce* (see *Salad Dressings*)
> water as needed

4. Process all ingredients together until creamy.

Assemble lasagna:

> 2–3 cups fresh spinach, washed and drained
> 1–2 cups organic button or shiitake
>   mushrooms, sliced
> 4–6 large super-ripe tomatoes, sliced

5. Layer zucchinis on bottom of pan being sure to drain off excess oil from marinade.

6. Next ladle marinara and cashew "ricotta" over the zucchini "noodles." Cover with handfuls of fresh spinach followed by a layer of mushrooms.

7. Top with sliced tomatoes.

8. Repeat all layers. Let flavors blend for one hour and then serve at room temperature.

Zucchini Angel Hair Pasta R

You need a **Veggie Spiralizer** machine* for this recipe. It is a wonderful, simple machine to use. By placing chunks of **zucchini** on the gripping prongs and closing the lid, one only needs to crank a handle located on the top and *wah-la!* Long threads of angel hair pasta appear in a receptacle bowl.

It is important to keep this device away from children as there are extremely sharp blades within the chambers that make for lovely cutting but could be horrific with little fingers. However, as long as there is an adult to supervise, this is safe and very fun. Kids love turning the crank and seeing the zucchini turn into pasta.

* To order a Veggie Spiralizer email me at:
   wrboyd@earthlink.net

RawSome Pesto Sauce ℞

> ³/4 cup organic olive oil
> 2–4 cloves garlic minced depending on taste

First blend above ingredients together. Then add:

> 4 T. of pine nuts that have soaked for at least 20 minutes, but not longer than one hour
> 1 cup chopped basil
> 2 tsp. apricot jam or 2–4 pitted dates, soaked
> 1–2 T. lemon juice
> Celtic Sea Salt to taste

Mix all in food processor.

Festive Pasta Platter ℞

> 2–4 zucchinis
> 2–4 yellow zucchini squash
> 1 batch *Raw Marinara Sauce* (see recipe this section)
> 1 batch *RawSome Pesto Sauce* (see recipe above)
> 1 cup macadamia nuts
> I bunch kale
> 3 ripe large tomatoes, diced

1. Find a large serving platter. The size and oval shape of a turkey platter works great for this. Arrange the kale leaves with stems pointing in towards the center all the way around the platter.

2. Using a **Veggie Spiralizer** machine,* first turn green zucchinis into angel hair pasta.

3. Mound a clump of zucchini pasta on center left of platter, leaving room on the center right section of the platter.

4. Repeat "spiralizing" production with yellow squash to yield angel hair pasta to place on the platter next to the green pasta.

5. Ladle *Raw Marinara* over the green pasta and *RawSome Pesto* over the yellow pasta.

6. Quickly process macadamia nuts using the pulse button. Be sure not to over-process, just breaking down the nuts small enough so they resemble parmesan cheese. Sprinkle pasta with "*parmesan.*"

7. Using diced tomatoes, make a border around the pasta.

* See information on Veggie Spiralizer on previous page.

oh spaghetti un-os *S*

RawSome Kid Recipe!

> 1 15oz. can organic tomato sauce (I recommend Trader Joe's)
> 1 tsp. garlic powder
> 1 tsp. honey or agave

Mix all ingredients in a sauce pan. Heat and serve over lentil pasta, quinoa pasta or organic whole wheat pasta (found in health food stores) or raw angel hair pasta (found and made fresh in your kitchen)!

Scrumptious Corn Bread *S*

RawSome Kid Recipe!

> ¼ cup agave or honey
> 1 cup plain rice, almond or grain milk
> 1 egg (or substitute ½ cup applesauce)
> 1 cup corn meal
> ½ cup whole wheat flour
> ½ cup ground flaxseeds
> 3 T. melted butter
> 2 tsp. baking powder
> ½ tsp. baking soda
> ½ tsp. *Gamazio* (see *Honorable Hors d'Oeuvres…*)

1. Beat egg, milk and agave or honey.

2. Mix all dry ingredients together.

3. Combine all plus melted butter.

4. Spread evenly into buttered 8 inch pan and bake at 350°. Check in 25 minutes.

Great with Pea Soup Duet!

Tasty Refried Beans for Tostadas, Tacos or Burritos S

2 cups dried pinto beans
3 carrots, sliced
2 pieces kombu
Celtic Sea Salt to taste
approx. 2 T. *Home Base Sauce,* (see *Salad Dressings*)
2 medium yellow onions, diced
3 chopped tomatoes

1. Soak pinto beans in enough boiling water to cover for two hours or just soak beans in cold water overnight. Drain.

2. Cook beans over medium heat in pot of water with carrots, kombu and salt to taste. Cook until beans are soft, between one and two hours depending on your heat source and how long the beans have soaked.

3. In a skillet, pour *Home Base Dressing* and add diced onions and chopped tomatoes. Sauté until the onions are soft and translucent.

4. While that is cooking, blend at least half of the cooked beans in blender and pour into skillet on top of onions and tomatoes.

5. Add remaining beans to skillet and refry until desired thickness is achieved.

Notes:

For a tostada, start with **organic corn tortillas** or **sprouted whole wheat tortillas.** Then add a layer of the beans with **romaine lettuce** shredded into small pieces. Top with **diced tomatoes, black olives** and **sliced avocados.** Use your favorite **salsa** as a dressing.

For tacos, use soft **organic corn tortillas.**

For burritos, try **sprouted whole wheat tortillas** (Trader Joe's carries these).

If you must use cheese, try grating **rennetless raw goat milk cheddar cheese,** made by Greenbank Farms.

Quinoa Delight *S*

1 onion, diced
5 or 6 shiitake mushrooms, cut into small pieces
a generous handful of string beans, cut into thirds (eliminate the tips first)
2 large stalks of broccoli, chopped
slivered almonds
1 cup quinoa
Home Base Sauce (see *Salad Dressings*)

1. Soak quinoa four to eight hours.

2. Drain and rinse.

3. Heat quinoa in 2 cups water just to boiling, then simmer over low heat until all water is absorbed. Be sure to check on it regularly, as it cooks in about 20–30 minutes.

4. Shake up *Home Base Sauce* and pour enough to coat a pan generously.

5. Sauté onions and mushrooms.

6. Once onions are soft, add green beans and broccoli.

7. Cover and cook on low until crisp and tender.

8. Turn off heat and add cooked quinoa to pan.

9. Toss. Serve with slivered almonds.

Notes:
Adding **feta** while all is still in the pan makes for a yummy creamier taste. Be sure to toss well.

Currants or **raisins** make a wonderful addition, and make this more kid-friendly.

Lemony Garlic Braised Greens S

snitchy bit of organic butter or organic olive oil
one diced red onion
1 cup finely chopped cloves of garlic
juice of two lemons
any combo of kale, collards, and chard, cut up into bite-size pieces

1. Sauté onion in butter or oil and add water if you wish.
2. Next add garlic and lemon juice, sautéing until garlic and onions have cooked well, adding water and more lemon juice as needed.
3. Wash but don't drain the greens and add to skillet.
4. Place a lid on the skillet and turn heat down to low. Cook until crisp and tender.

Option:
Serve with fresh raw corn on the cob!

Lemony Scalloped Potatoes S

RawSome Kid Recipe!

4 russet potatoes
1 cup broth
2 sweet onions
10 cloves garlic, quartered
$\frac{1}{2}$ cup lemon juice
4 T. olive oil
1 tsp. basil
Celtic Sea Salt
garlic salt
$\frac{1}{2}$ cup organic parmesan cheese (optional)

1. Skin and thinly slice potatoes.
2. Blanch potatoes in boiling water for 5 minutes.
3. Sauté onions and garlic in broth.
4. Layer onions and blanched potato slices.
5. Sprinkle with garlic salt and parmesan cheese.
6. Mix lemon juice, oil, basil and salt.
7. Pour lemon/oil mix over potatoes.
8. Bake at 375° for 1½ hours.

Robyn's Roast Potato Medley S

an assortment of potatoes like yellow fin, Yukon gold, red and purple potatoes
(enough to fill a roasting pan full)
approximately ½ cup of *Home Base Sauce* (see *Salad Dressings*)
2 red onions, diced
10–20 cloves garlic, peeled
2 heaping T. apricot jam
garlic salt and[or Celtic Sea Salt
Tony's or any Italian seasoning

1. Pour enough *Home Base Sauce* to cover bottom of a large skillet. Add apricot jam,which will make the sauce more like a glaze to caramelize the onions in. Sauté onions until translucent.

2. Thoroughly wash and cut potatoes into quarters (or smaller, if potatoes are large).

3. Place potatoes in large roasting pan and pour onions on top. Add seasoning and garlic cloves and toss potatoes until well coated.

4. Add more *Home Base Sauce* if needed. Bake at 375° until crisp and potatoes are soft.

Jasmine Rice with Asparagus & Shiitake Mushrooms S

jasmine rice (available at Trader Joe's or health food stores)
½–1 tsp. nutmeg
Home Base Sauce (see *Salad Dressings*)
healthy bunch of asparagus, sliced
2–3 ripe tomatoes, diced
1 tsp. *Gamazio* (see *Honorable Hors d'Oeuvres…*)
8–10 shiitake mushrooms, sliced
chopped almonds

1. Rinse rice thoroughly and follow cooking directions on package, adding ½–1 tsp. of nutmeg to the water to permeate the rice while cooking. This rice cooks very quickly, so be sure to watch it and keep the heat on low.

2. While rice is cooking, sauté shiitake mushrooms in *Home Base Sauce*.

3. When mushrooms are soft, add sliced-up asparagus and cook only long enough to be crisp and tender.

4. Meanwhile, as asparagus finishes up, add two or three diced ripe tomatoes plus 1 tsp. *Gamazio* to rice once it is done cooking.

5. Place rice on a large serving dish. Cover with mushrooms and asparagus.

6. Top this dish off with a generous amount of chopped almonds.

Serve with a large salad and enjoy a tasty dinner!

Brown Rice & Veggies with Purple Confetti S

> 1 cup brown rice
> 2 cups water
> 1 strip of kombu seaweed
> 2–4 cloves garlic

1. Cook one cup rice in two cups water. Snip up kombu into little pieces with kitchen scissors and add to rice as it begins to cook. Also throw in several cloves of garlic.

2. Use enough **Home Base Sauce** (see _Salad Dressings_) to sauté the following:

> 6 shiitake mushrooms, sliced
> 3 medium tomatoes, chopped
> 1 yellow onion, diced
> 1 red onion, diced
> 1 bunch broccoli
> 2 small zucchinis, sliced

3. After all veggies are cooked crisp tender, turn off heat and add **Tahini Dressing**.

Tahini Dressing

> 1 cup lemon juice
> 1 cup water
> 1 cup raw tahini butter
> 2 cloves garlic
> 1/2 cup onion, chopped
> 1 tsp. honey, agave or maple syrup

4. Blend all ingredients.

5. Toss with veggies and top with homemade **Gamazio** (see _Honorable Hors d'Oeuvres…_).

6. Decorate outside edge of plate with **purple cabbage** confetti by taking cabbage and processing with "S" blade into fine confetti-like pieces.

Option:
Along with onion, garlic, shiitake mushrooms, tomatoes and zucchinis, stir fry **sliced carrots**, and **frozen peas**. Crumble **organic feta cheese** on top and serve with salad.

Lovely Lentil, Millet & Nut Loaf S

This is a lovely mock meat loaf that can be served with mushroom gravy. Works great for special occasions and holiday dinners.

> 1¼ cups lentils
> 1 cup millet
> 1 or 2 red onions
> 1-2 T. organic butter or olive oil
> ¾ cup chopped walnuts (or you can use pecans or almonds instead)
> 1 can (14.5oz.) organic diced tomatoes with basil
> Erewhon's Barley Plus cooked cereal (or use 1 cup cooked oatmeal)
> 1 tsp. cumin
> 1 tsp. garlic powder
> Celtic Sea Salt to taste
> parsley flakes, oregano, rosemary, sage, basil, or thyme as desired

1. Cook lentils in enough water to cover until tender, then pour into a colander to drain off all the liquid.

2. Cook millet in **2 cups of water** (takes about 25 minutes when cooked on simmer).

3. Drain all liquid from diced tomatoes. ***The key to a successful loaf is not too much moisture!***

4. Sauté onions in organic butter or olive oil.

5. Follow directions for Erewhon's Barley Plus cooked cereal and make enough for 2 servings (or use 1 cup cooked oatmeal)

6. Mix all ingredients together.

7. Using a small amount of organic butter, grease a loaf pan and press mixture firmly in place. Bake for 45 minutes at 350°.

Option:
Pour tomato sauce or marinara sauce on top of loaf and then bake. Or simply place sliced tomatoes on top of loaf.

Notes:
Serve with **Garlic Mashed Cauliflower** (see recipe next page) and **Wholly Gravy** (see *Honorable Hors d'Oeuvres…*).

If you have mixture left over, form into patties and bake on a cookie sheet for great veggie burgers.

Sliced loaf makes great leftovers, or filling for sandwiches. Also nice served cold on a fresh salad.

Kids like to use fruit-juice sweetened **organic ketchup** on this! Freezes well.

Garlic Mashed Cauliflower *or Beyond Mashed Potatoes!* S

(Inspired by Lori Johnson)

> 2 heads cauliflower
> ¼ cup organic olive oil
> 1 small clove garlic or ½ tsp. garlic powder
> salt to taste
> any herbs or spices you like on mashed potatoes
> organic butter
> small amount of plain rice milk or water

1. Steam cauliflower until soft and tender.

2. Place all ingredients in processor and add small amounts of rice milk or water until cauliflower resembles mashed potatoes. A real crowd pleaser!

Butternut Squash, Kale & White Beans S

> 1 bunch of kale, cut into small pieces
> 1 small red onion, diced
> 1 large butternut squash
> 2 cups white beans
> 2 carrots, sliced
> 3 stalks celery, sliced
> salt
> garlic powder
> 2 T. *Home Base Sauce* (see *Salad Dressings*)
> 1 can of salt-free diced stewing tomatoes
> 1 T. olive oil

1. Measure out 2 cups beans and place in pot. Add 6 cups of water and throw in carrots, celery, garlic powder and salt to taste. Cook until beans are tender.

2. While beans cook, steam the squash until tender.

3. Next, sauté red onions in *Home Base Sauce*.

4. After onions are soft, add kale and cover with a lid. Turn heat down and sauté until kale is tender.

5. In a skillet, heat olive oil and add stewing tomatoes.

6. Remove outer skin of butternut squash and cut into small chunks.

7. Add to the tomatoes. Cook only long enough to mix the two together to warm all the way through.

8. Using a slotted spoon, remove three or four spoonfuls of cooked beans, including as many pieces of carrots and celery as possible. Blend in a processor or blender with a small amount of cook water. Drain the remaining beans carrots and celery and discard the cook water. Add blended beans back into whole beans. Season to taste.

9. On a plate or in a bowl, begin with a portion of kale to form the bottom layer. Next add a layer of the tomato and squash mixture, and finally a topping of beans.

Mashed Parsnips & Yams S

4 large garnet yams
2 large parsnips

1. Wash and cut up yams and parsnips (leaving skin on).
2. Steam yams and parsnips until very soft.
3. Remove skins from yams once they cool down a bit.
4. Whip yams and parsnips in processor.

Option:
Use **organic butter** and **seasonings** to taste.

Mock Tuna Melts S

(Lisa Silva took the Mock Tuna recipe and turned it into these melt sandwiches!)

1 cup each sunflower seeds and almonds soaked
1/4 cup brown sesame seeds soaked
1/2 cup celery, chopped very fine
1/2 cup fresh parsley, finely snipped
1/3 cup purified water
1/4 cup fresh lemon juice
1 tsp. onion powder
1 tsp. kelp granules
1 tsp. garlic powder
fresh sliced tomato
sunflower sprouts
Vegenaise
sprouted wheat buns
Greenbank Farms raw cheddar goat cheese

1. Soak nuts and seeds for 3 hours and let drain for 8 hours (or overnight).
2. Begin mixing parsley, lemon juice, water and seasonings in a food processor or blender.
3. Add nuts, seeds and celery.
4. Use enough Vegenaise mayo to blend as if tuna.
5. Scoop a generous amount onto a sprouted wheat bun (Trader Joe's carries these). You can use **mustard** or mayo on the bun if you like.
6. Top with slices of raw goat cheese. Place this along with the top half of bun in toaster oven until cheese melts. You may need to take the top bun out before the cheese melts on the other half, so it doesn't get over-toasted.
7. Top with fresh tomato slice and sunflower sprouts.

Honorable Hors d'Oeuvres, Condiments & Snackies!

Raw

Some

Photo: RawSome Hummus (page 130)

Thai Appetizer R

    1 lime
    fresh ginger the size of your thumb
    ½ cup shredded coconut
    8 unsulfered dried apricots, soaked for 4 hours
    3 small pitted dates, soaked for 4 hours
    2–4 T. apricot/date soak water
    ½ cup ground up macadamia nuts
    ½ large red onion, diced small
    ½ cucumber, diced very small
    approx. 1cup large fresh spinach leaves
    1 tsp. Nama shoyu
    ½ tsp. garlic powder
    1–2 tsp. honey (start with one and adjust to taste)

Note: Ideally it is nice to serve the ingredients in small round glass serving dishes or little white custard cups. Use one serving dish for every separate item.*

1. Soak apricots and dates together in enough water to cover for four hours. Drain, saving soak water.

2. Cut the lime in half and juice only one half. Slice the other half in half again and then make very thin slices. This will give you small triangle wedges. Cut each wedge into thirds, leaving the peel intact. It is the peel that adds so much to the overall taste of this dish.

3. Now cut the ginger into thin strips about 3/4 inch long.

4. Place sliced ginger, coconut, macadamia nuts and diced cucumber into small separate dishes or bowls (see note above).

5. In a food processor, mix the apricots, dates, honey, garlic powder, shoyu and the lime juice you have set aside. Add one tablespoon at a time of the apricot/date soak water until the consistency is similar to plum sauce (usually about 3 tablespoons). Don't make it too watery. **Note:** If you are in a hurry you can use **organic fruit-juice sweetened apricot jam** in place of the soaked apricots and dates.

6. Put the apricot sauce into a slightly larger round dish.

7. On a tray or in a large flat basket, arrange all the dishes in a circle. Place the apricot sauce in the middle. If you have enough room on your serving platter, lay out the spinach leaves. Otherwise display them on a separate plate. Put tiny serving spoons into each dish.

8. Begin assembling by holding a spinach leaf in the palm of your hand like you would a tortilla. First place a piece of lime, then a strip of ginger. Spoon on some onions and cucumbers, then sprinkle on some macadamia nuts and coconut. Finally, top with apricot sauce. Eat it taco style and enjoy the zesty surprise of the combination of these tastes.

*See photo of recipe on title page of book.

Young Coconut Meat, Heirloom Tomatoes & Basil   R

1 young coconut
fresh basil leaves
¼ cup organic olive oil
assortment of your favorite heirloom tomatoes, including the orange,
    green and yellow ones
1 basket of orange cherry tomatoes
½ red onion diced
2 cloves garlic
½ tsp. salt
1 lemon
3–4 ripe green tomatoes

1. Using the pulse setting, process olive oil, garlic, salt and 6 large leaves of basil. Pulse about a half dozen times to mix ingredients and chop up the garlic. Using a spatula, scrape the oil blend into a large shallow serving dish.

2. Cut the heirloom tomatoes into slices and then in half again, making half moons. Slice as many cherry tomatoes as you like in half. Let the tomatoes marinate in the basil oil while you continue preparing.

3. Cut up onions and toss in with tomatoes.

4. Stack 6 large basil leaves on top of each other. Tightly roll entire stack from small tip of leaf to stem. Holding the leaves down and tight with one hand, slice the entire roll into strips. As the leaves unfold you should now have long thin strips to scatter on the tomatoes. Repeat the entire process again. Do more if you want more basil than this.

5. Hack open the coconut. Pour out the water and reserve for drinking or other uses. Scoop out the young coconut meat and cut into small pieces mocking Mozzarella cheese.

6. Add the coconut to the bowl and toss everything together well. Taste and adjust salt if necessary.

7. Wash the outer skin of the lemon. Slice lemon in half, then cut each piece into half moons. Arrange around the outer edge of bowl with the skin edge up and the flat edge down.

8. Slice the green tomatoes and use to decorate outer edge of bowl, alternating with the lemons.

Cucumber Chips with Ranchy Almond Spread ℞

> 3 T. Udo's Oil
> juice of 1 lemon
> 2 cloves of garlic, minced
> ½–1 cup grapeseed Vegenaise
> touch of honey
> ½–¾ cup almonds, soaked overnight then rinsed and drained
> 6 sundried tomatoes, soaked for several hours
> 1 sheet nori seaweed
> kelp granules
> 1 long English cucumber
> optional: 1 tsp. dried onion flakes

1. Process lemon juice, honey, two sundried tomatoes and garlic first.

2. Start by adding ½ cup each mayo and almonds and process everything together. You may need to add more almonds and/or mayo until you get a nice spreadable paté consistency.

3. Wash cucumber. Using a crinkle cutter if you have one, slice cucumber on the diagonal to make large cucumber chips.

4. Spoon almond spread on top of each cucumber slice.

5. Drain sundried tomatoes and cut into tiny pieces. Decorate the slices with the tomato pieces.

6. Cut very thin ½ strips of nori and decorate the top with vertical strips. Sprinkle with kelp. Serve on platter.

Options:

Instead of the sundried tomatoes and nori, chop up some **olives** and top the paté with that.

You can also make up some **Gorgeous Guacamole** (see recipe this section) and top every other cucumber chip with that.

Acorn Grapes with Ranchy Almond Spread ℞

RawSome Kid Recipe!

> 1 cup ranchy almond spread
> 1 cup finely chopped walnuts or pecans
> 1 bunch of red seedless organic grapes

1. Follow steps 1–3 above and make the *Ranchy Almond Spread* thick enough to dip the plump end of a grape into and have the spread stick.

2. Spread the nuts out on a plate and roll the same plump end of the grape into the chopped nuts covering the spread. Arrange the grapes, which now look like acorns, on a platter and serve.

Summer Island Dip or Dressing ℞

Good on salads or as a dip for fresh cut-up veggies.

¼ cup olive oil
2 cloves garlic
1 tsp. fruit-sweetened apricot jam or 1–2 pitted medjool dates
1 large ripe tomato
½ red bell pepper
3 T. brown rice vinegar

Blenderize or food process all ingredients.

Cashew Paté ℞

A real party pleaser!

1 cup cashews
1 cup sunflower seeds
approx. 16 oz. of your favorite salsa (or 16-oz. jar Muir Glen Organic Mild or Medium Salsa)

1. Place ½ cup each of cashews and sunflower seeds in processor. Grind to a fine meal. Add the second half of each and repeat.

2. Slowly add salsa until the consistency is moist but stiff enough to spread as paté.

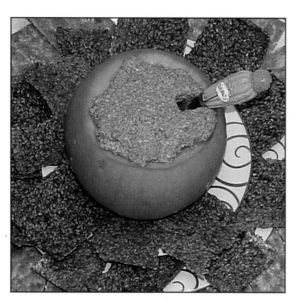

Notes:

This paté is great served on raw **flaxseed crackers** (see recipes on following pages). Or serve with store-bought crackers—my favorites are **Ak-mak** crackers; they go really well with this. (Ak-mak can be found at Trader Joe's or most health food stores).

Around holiday time, it is fun to serve this inside a scooped-out mini **pumpkin**. Line the inside of the pumpkin with brown wax paper, which will act as a barrier so the pumpkin flavor doesn't disturb the paté flavor.

Paté tastes best when chilled first. It tastes even better the next day, so it is great to make ahead. If stored in the refrigerator in a tightly sealed container, this will keep at least three days.

Sundried Tomato Flaxseed Crackers R

NOTE: dehydrator needed

> **2 cups flaxseeds, soaked 2–6 hours**
> **1 cup sundried tomatoes, soaked at least 4 hours**
> **3 cloves garlic**
> **2 T. onion flakes**
> **2 T. Italian seasoning**
> **1 T. garlic powder**

1. Purée soaked tomatoes with enough soak water to make a paste.

2. Add fresh garlic, onion flakes, garlic powder and Italian seasoning. You will notice that the soaked flax is now a gelatinous batter. Mix it in as is.

3. Spread on teflex sheets and score into five even vertical rows using a spatula. Next, score horizontal rows according to the size you want your crackers.

4. Place in dehydrator and set temperature at 105°. Re-score your rows after one hour of dehydrating. Return one hour later and re-score again. Let dehydrate until the crackers are crisp, turning them once after 12 hours. Remove the teflex sheet when you turn crackers over to dehydrate the second side (see directions on how to do this under _Sweet Corn Crackers_ recipe this section). Dehydration can take anywhere from 24–36 hours, depending on outside temperature and humidity.

5. Store in air tight Mason jars. If they get a little stale, you can try dehydrating them again—this usually perks them up again!

Flax to the Max Crackers! ℞

NOTE: dehydrator needed

    2 cups flaxseeds, soaked 2–6 hours
    1½ cups almonds, soaked 6–12 hours
    2 cups carrot pulp or finely grated carrots (approximately 4 large carrots)
    2 stalks celery (cut each stalk in half for best food processing)
    1 medium red bell pepper, sliced into quarters (ready for the processor)
    ½ red onion or a sweet Maui onion
    ½ cup fresh cilantro
    3 T. olive oil
    4 pitted dates, soaked for at least an hour
    2 T. fresh lemon juice
    2 cloves garlic
    ½–1 tsp. curry powder
    ½ tsp. cumin
    ¼ tsp. tumeric
    ½–1 tsp. ginger powder
    1½ tsp. Real Salt
    ½ tsp. red pepper flakes
    1 tsp. honey or agave

1. Put carrots and almonds through a juicer using the blank plate. Dump into a large bowl.

2. In food processor, mix oil and garlic cloves.

3. Add lemon juice, honey and all spices (for more of a kick to the taste, add more spices, especially the curry and red pepper flakes) and blend until integrated.

4. Add the dates and continue to blend until mixture becomes a moist paste.

5. Continue by adding the onion, celery and red bell peppers. Make sure these veggies are pre-cut small enough so they will blend nicely in the processor.

6. Add the carrot and almond pulp into the processor and blend everything together thoroughly.

7. Dump the contents of the processor back into the large bowl and finally add the soaked flaxseeds. (They will have absorbed all the water and become quite gelatinous). Use your hands to mix everything together well.

8. Using a spatula, spread cracker batter on teflex sheet approximately ¼-inch thick.

9. Score crackers with tip of spatula and dehydrate at 105° for 6–8 hours. Turn crackers over, removing the teflex sheet (see directions on how to do this under *Sweet Corn Crackers* recipe this section), Continue dehydrating for 12 more hours or until the crackers are very crisp. Store in glass Mason jars. Makes approximately three trays worth! *Enjoy flax to the max!*

Sweet Corn Crackers R

NOTE: dehydrator needed

> 5 large ears of fresh sweet corn, removed from cob
> 3/4 cup sunflower seeds, soaked 4–6 hours
> 3/4 cup almonds, soaked overnight and blanched
> 2 T. pine nuts, soaked two hours
> 2 T. golden flaxseeds, ground into powder
> 1 small sweet yellow onion, diced (Maui or Walla Walla)
> 1½ –2 tsp. salt or *Gamazio* (see recipe this section)

1. Begin by draining the nuts and seeds, keeping the almonds separate.

2. Boil water and pour into a bowl. Blanche the almonds by dropping them in the bowl of boiling water for 20 seconds and then add cold water until the water temperature is reduced to warm. Pinch each almond between your thumb and forefinger and pop off the skins.

3. Process all the nuts and seeds in the food processor. Transfer nuts and seeds into a bowl.

4. Next process the corn.

5. In a coffee grinder or high-powered blender, grind the flaxseeds into a fine powder and add to the corn. Process the two together.

6. Now add the onion and the salt or *Gamazio*.

7. Add the processed nuts and seeds in with the corn mixture and process until everything has been thoroughly blended together.

8. Place teflex sheets on two trays. Divide the batter in half. Drop half of the batter into the center of the first sheet and spread it evenly to all four edges using a spatula (approximately ¼-inch thick). Score into rows vertically and then horizontally to create crackers of any size you like. Repeat the process on the second tray.

9. Dehydrate for 12–14 hours at 105°. Remove tray and place another tray over it upside down (no teflex sheet). Now the second tray is now upside down on top of the tray of crackers. Flip everything over and carefully peel away the teflex sheet as you press the crackers into place on the fresh (screen only) tray. Continue dehydrating for another 18 hours or until the crackers are nice and crisp.

Option:
Sprinkle **white sesame seeds** on top. Also try adding diced **red bell peppers.**

RawSome Hummus R

(This recipe requires prepping three days in advance!)

> **2 cups dried garbanzo beans, soaked 2 hours**

1. Rinse thoroughly and leave to sprout for three days, making sure to rinse and drain at least three times a day.

    > **juice of one large lemon (more if you like stronger lemon flavor)**
    > **2–4 cloves garlic, minced**
    > **¼ to ½ cup raw tahini (again, add more if you like stronger flavor)**
    > **2 T. organic olive oil**
    > **½ to 1 tsp. raw honey**
    > **Celtic Sea Salt to taste**

2. Mix above ingredients thoroughly in food processor and then add:

    > **½ cup purified water**
    > **sprouted garbanzo beans (they should have little tails)**

3. Squeeze a little lemon juice on top and garnish with parsley. Serve with raw veggies or pita bread cut in triangles.

Options:

Add a can of **organic garbanzo beans** to smooth out the taste and texture.

For a festive holiday twist, mix in fresh snipped **chives** and top with **pomegranate seeds.**

Garnish with a few **dried persimmons.**

Mango Tango Salsa R

RawSome Kid Recipe!

(Not the greatest food combination but fun as a treat occasionally)

> one package frozen mangos from Trader Joe's, thawed
> one fresh mango (or just use 3 fresh mangos total)
> juice from one or two limes
> 1/2–3/4 cup red bell pepper, diced
> 1 fresh Anaheim chili, diced (or 1 can of mild green chilies)
> corn off one large cob
> one bunch of cilantro finely chopped
> 1/2 red onion finely chopped
> Celtic Sea Salt to taste
> one avocado, diced

Mix all together and chill. Serve with vegetable slices and guacamole, or use as a condiment.

Salsa Way Fresca R

1. Mix the following in a food processor:

    > 1/2 sweet yellow onion and 1/2 red onion
    > 1 bunch of cilantro
    > juice of 1 lemon and 1 lime
    > 10–12 cloves garlic
    > Celtic Sea Salt

2. Then add:

    > 8–12 really ripe tomatoes

3. Transfer to a bowl and add in:

    > 1/2 jicama, diced in small chunks
    > 1 red bell pepper, diced
    > fresh Anaheim or jalapeno peppers, diced fine (only if you want heat)

Gorgeous Guacamole R

RawSome Kid Recipe!

1. Put the meat of **three ripe avocados** in food processor with:

   > **juice of one lemon**
   > **Celtic Sea Salt to taste**
   > **2 or 3 cloves garlic**

2. Blend just long enough to mix everything but not long enough to make it too smooth.
3. Remove and place in mixing bowl.
4. Add:

   > **1 tomato, diced**
   > **1 more avocado, diced small**
   > **½ red onion, diced (more if desired)**
   > **diced fresh cilantro**

Jicama Lemon Sticks R

> **1 jicama, peeled and cut into sticks**
> **juice of one lemon**
> **Wholearth Spice Latin America blend (www.wholearthspice.com) or cayenne pepper.**

Marinate all ingredients together and refrigerate. Great to use as dipping sticks with the *Gorgeous Guacamole* above.

Gamazio Condiment R

1. Grind 1 cup of **sesame seeds** in a coffee grinder.
2. Place in food processor and add 1–2 heaping T. of **Celtic Sea Salt** (or to taste).
3. Pour into a bowl and mix in 1–2 T. of **whole white sesame seeds**.
   Pour into a salt shaker or store in a glass jar.

Option:
Try adding some **kelp granules**.

Sprouted Lentils as a Condiment R

1. Cover ¾ cup of dried **lentils** in water 2–3 hours.

2. Drain through a small mesh stainless colander. I found the perfect colanders for sprouting at Cost Plus Imports. They are all wire mesh and come in nice small, medium and larger sizes.

3. Set the lentils in the colander at an angle over a dish-drying rack so it can drain further.

4. A couple of times a day stop by and rinse your growing sprouts (at least once in the morning and once at night). They will grow tails in about a day.

5. Transfer them to a glass container and store them in the fridge.

6. If you take them out and rinse them daily, they will last about 3 days.

Notes:
Use them as a condiment to add to soups, salads, sandwiches, or on top of rice. They are also a nice take-along munchie snack. Sprouted lentils are full of enzymes and are one of those live foods bursting with vital nutrients!

Sunflower Seed Sprouts R

Sprouted sunflower seeds are my favorite sprouts. Although I personally don't grow these, I buy them several times a week at the health food store as well as the farmers market. They are so wonderful on salads and especially good on sandwiches and stuffed in pita pockets.

Often kids will eat these when they don't usually like sprouts. We like to nibble on these as a snack food, too!

Buckwheat Bits R

2 cups buckwheat groats, soaked overnight

1. Rinse and drain groats.

2. Place a teflex sheet on a tray and spread groats out as much as possible, avoiding clumping.

3. Dehydrate 15–24 hours or until they are crunchy.

Use in place of bacon bits. Great on salads.

Honey Coconut Butter R

RawSome Kid Recipe!

> **4 T. coconut oil**
> **4 T. honey or agave**
> **1½ tsp. cinnamon**
> **½ tsp. salt**

In a processor or blender, mix the coconut oil, honey, cinnamon and salt. Use like you would honey butter.

This is great on toast. Kids love it!

Garlicky Better Butter R

> **1 cube organic butter**
> **4 T. Udo's Oil or organic olive oil (or half and half)**
> **2 cloves garlic**
> **fresh herbs of your choice (optional)**

In a processor, whip all ingredients together.

Great on homemade bread or *Brown Rice Muffins* (see recipe this section)!

Honey 'N Nuts Munchie Mix R

NOTE: dehydrator needed

> **1 cup almonds soaked overnight**
> **½ cup macadamia nuts, soaked 2 hours**
> **½ cup pecans, soaked 2 hours**
> **½ walnuts, soaked 1 hour**
> **2 T. coconut oil**
> **2 T. honey or agave**
> **1½ tsp. cinnamon**
> **1 tsp. salt**

1. Drain all nuts well and pat dry with a towel to remove as much excess moisture as possible.

2. In a processor or blender, mix the coconut oil, honey, cinnamon and salt.

3. Put the nuts into a large mixing bowl and pour the blended ingredients on top. Using clean hands, mix the nuts thoroughly, making sure to coat them evenly. Using a teflex sheet, spread mixture out on a tray and dehydrate at 105° for 8 hours. Remove the teflex sheet and dehydrate another 12–14 hours. This is a great snack for road trips, lunch boxes or after school.

Holiday Assortment Tray R

(*Inspired by Duffy Grant*)

> pistachio nuts
> dried persimmons
> coconut date rolls
> *Honey 'N Nuts Munchie Mix* or almonds
> fresh rosemary sprigs

1. Use the rosemary to form a dividing cross on your circular platter. The rosemary adds a wonderful festive aroma to this presentation.

2. Arrange all ingredients as shown in the picture.

Fernando's Fabulous Mango Salsa S

RawSome Kid Recipe!

> 2–3 large mangos, diced small
> 3 red bell peppers
> 2 small red Fresno chili peppers
> fresh cilantro
> fresh mint
> 2 T. olive oil
> juice of 1/2 lemon
> 1 1/2 capfuls of brown rice vinegar
> salt to taste

1. Slice the bell pepper into lengthwise quarters. Slice the chili peppers in half and remove all seeds. Place the peppers skin side up on a cookie sheet and bake at 400° for about thirty minutes or until the outer skins become slightly blackened.

2. Remove from oven and immediately place in a bowl or jar that has a lid. Set on counter. This will create moisture inside the container making the removal of the skin extremely easy.

3. Cut the mango into chunks and place in a large bowl.

4. Chop up equal amounts of enough cilantro and mint to loosely fill a cup.

5. Combine all ingredients, except for the peppers, and mix.

6. Now de-skin the peppers.

7. Finely chop only the small chili pepper, then use the back of your knife to mash the pepper into a paste. Add about 1–2 teaspoons of this paste into the mango mixture to add a little zip.

8. Dice the red bell pepper, add to the salsa, and stir.

Notes:

Great served with fish. Great served with *anything!* This disappears really fast at our house!

Eager to Please Eggplant *S*

large eggplant
basil
2 lemons
3 cloves garlic
1/4 cup tahini

1. Bake one large eggplant, skin and all, at 400° for 45 minutes–1 hour.

2. Scoop out the eggplant meat and discard the skin.

3. Place all ingredients in blender.

Serve as a side dish or with **pita bread** as an appetizer.

Dan the Man's Bean Dip or Dressing *S*

About 16 oz cooked white beans (two cans organic white beans, rinsed and drained)
2 bunches cilantro
8 cloves garlic
juice of two lemons
olive oil to cover bottom of food processor
Celtic Sea Salt to taste
kelp granules

1. Blend all in processor.

2. For salad dressing, thin with water to desired consistency.

3. You can store in fridge for at least 5 days.

Green Beans in Raspberry Vinaigrette *S*

lots of fresh, raw green beans
10 cloves garlic, chopped
2 T. *Home Base Sauce* (see *Salad Dressings*)
1/3 cup sesame seeds
small red onion, diced fine
1/2 cup slivered almonds
1/2 cup Spectrum Naturals Raspberry Vinaigrette

1. Sauté onions and garlic in *Home Base Sauce*.

2. In a large bowl, mix all other ingredients.

3. When garlic and onions are cooked, allow to cool. Then mix in with everything else and toss thoroughly.

4. Serve on a nice platter. Sprinkle with extra sesame seeds.

Pesto-Veggie Sauce *S*

> 1 yellow onion, diced
> 1 golden zucchini
> ½ cup broth

1. Sauté onion and zucchini in ½ cup broth.
2. Add *RawSome Pesto Sauce* or pesto of your choice.

Notes:

Pour over **baked potatoes** and serve with salad for a great, but simple delicious meal!

Also good served over **steamed veggies** and **brown rice!**

Asparagus with Mustard Vinaigrette *S*

RawSome Kid Recipe!

A great appetizer

> 1 lb. asparagus, trimmed
> 2 T. pineapple juice
> 1 tsp. Dijon mustard
> 1 T. apple cider vinegar
> 1 tsp. olive oil or Udo's Oil
> 1 clove garlic, chopped

1. Steam asparagus until tender but still crisp and drain.
2. Combine remaining ingredients in shallow, non-metallic dish.
3. Add asparagus, turning to coat evenly. Cover and chill 1 hour.

Brown Rice Muffins *S*

RawSome Kid Recipe!

       1 cup cold cooked brown rice
       1¼ cup whole wheat flour
       2 heaping tsp. baking powder
       ½ tsp. Celtic Sea Salt
       2 tsp. honey
       2 organic eggs
       1 cup almond, rice or grain milk
       4 T. melted butter

1. Combine flour, baking powder and salt.

2. Combine eggs, honey, milk, butter, and rice.

3. Quickly combine the two mixtures. Don't over-beat.

4. Pour into lightly buttered muffin tins.

5. Bake at 425° for 20 to 25 minutes or until lightly browned. Cut into squares when done.

Option:

This is sooo delicious! Sauté **one onion**, diced small, in the 4 T. of melted butter that the recipes calls for. Once onions are cooked, scrape them along with the butter into the batter. Add two additional lightly beaten **egg whites** to batter. Continue recipe as above from Step 4.

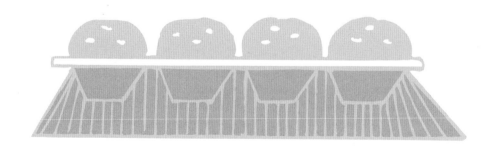

wholly Gravy *S*

RawSome Kid Recipe!

Great over baked potatoes.

1. Melt **3 T. butter.**
2. Sauté **½ cup chopped onions.**
3. Add and cook for three minutes:

     3 T. whole wheat pastry flour
     2 T. nutritional yeast
     ¼ tsp. thyme
     ½ tsp. garlic powder
     ½ tsp. Celtic Sea Salt

4. Slowly whisk in 1½ cups **purified water** and keep stirring on a very low heat until smooth and desired thickness is achieved. You may need to add more water. Adjust seasonings to taste.

Option:

Sauté **¾ cup sliced mushrooms** with the onions in butter. Set aside. Make gravy, using a wire whisk to smooth out any lumps. If gravy becomes very lumpy, you can transfer into a blender or processor to smooth. Return to pan and add onions and mushrooms. Can be reheated.

Homemade Croutons *S*

     Ezekiel and rye bread
     4 T. Home Base Sauce (see *Salad Dressings*)
     12 cloves garlic, chopped fine

1. Using an assortment of your favorite healthy breads, cut approximately 10 pieces into cubes. I like to use **Ezekiel with Sesame Seeds** and **yeast-free rye bread.** Using different lighter and darker colored bread makes for more gourmet-looking croutons.
2. Chop at least a dozen cloves of garlic and sauté in *Home Base Sauce.*
3. Add the cubed bread and cook over medium heat tossing so as to coat the bread and allow the sauce to be absorbed. Don't let it burn. Add more sauce if needed but don't drench. This is a fairly quick flash in the pan.
4. Transfer into a large enamel (if you have one) baking pan and bake at 425° for about 10 minutes. Try to turn pieces over and bake till golden brown. *Wa-la*, croutons!

Good on soups and always great on salads!

Rawsome Treats!

Raw

Some

Photo: Raw Fruit Tart (page 146)

Coconut Applesauce ℝ

2 apples
1 tsp. cinnamon
½ tsp. vanilla
3 room temperature dates
fresh coconut water

Mix all ingredients together in processor adding small amounts of coconut water as needed.

RawSome Apricot & Peach Cobbler ℝ

Crust

2 batches of leftover pulp from *Almond Milk* (see *Breakfasts & Beverages*)
6 pitted dates, soaked (save soak water)
½ cup raisins, soaked
¼ cup honey
¼ tsp. almond extract oil
handful of oats

1. Mix all ingredients except oats together in food processor.
2. Slowly add date-soak water as needed, until you get a nice firm but pliable crust.
3. Press crust batter into a pie pan, building it up along the side walls. Reserve handful of crust batter for crumble topping.

Purée

1 cup dried apricots, soaked in 1 cup orange juice overnight
zest of one orange

4. Pureé apricots, OJ soak and zest in food processor.
5. Spread apricot mix on top of crust reserving ¼ of the total amount of crust for topping.
6. Slice 4–6 peaches and place on top of apricot spread.
7. Take remaining crust batter and process with handful of oats, then crumble over peaches.

Whipped Cashew Cream Topping

1½ cup cashews, soaked
3 pitted dates, soaked
½ cup fresh OJ

8. Process soaked cashews and dates with OJ. You can add **Almond Milk*** or **water** if you need to.
9. Adding **a few drops of vanilla** is nice. For a creamier whip, add less orange juice and more almond milk.

Raw Banana Coconut Cream Pie R

½ cup almonds, soaked overnight
7–8 very ripe large bananas
2 heaping T. almond butter
½ cup shredded coconut
1½ cups oats
½ cup currants
1 tsp. cinnamon
2 tsp. vanilla

Crust

1. Process five of the bananas with almond butter and coconut. Set aside half of this mixture.
2. Mix the other half with oats, almonds, currants and cinnamon. You may need to add more oats and/or almond butter until you find the right consistency, and press into a pie pan for crust.

Filling

3. Slice up two or three bananas and arrange on the bottom of pie crust so they crowd each other.
4. Pour the reserved banana almond cream over bananas and dust with coconut.

Serve with a glass of Almond Milk (see recipe in Breakfasts & Beverages)!

Macadamia Coconut Cheesecake R

1½ cups macadamia nuts, soaked in coconut water
11 dates at room temperature
meat from two coconuts
½ cup coconut water
½ cup shredded coconut dried
¼ cup macadamia nuts
fresh grated vanilla bean
1 large ripe mango
½ banana

Crust

1. After opening two coconuts and setting aside ½ cup coconut water (to use for the filling), use the remaining coconut water to soak 1½ cups of macadamia nuts for 1 hour.
2. Process the drained nuts with 7 dates and press dough into pie pan.

Filling

3 Process all other ingredients and spread over crust.
4. Refrigerate for several hours so the cheesecake will set.
5. In a processor pulse one ripe mango with ½ banana and spread as a topping.

RawSome Carrot Cake ℝ

RawSome Kid Recipe!

(Inspired by a recipe by Rose Lee Calabro)

> 6 cups carrots
> 1 cup almonds, soaked overnight
>   (or use pulp from *Almond Milk,* in *Breakfasts & Beverages*)
> 1½ cups walnuts, soaked, overnight
> 1 cup shredded coconut
> 1 cup currants
> 1 cup medjool or honey dates, pitted
> 2 tsp. vanilla
> 1 tsp. cinnamon
> 1 heaping T. psyllium powder
> juice of 1 lemon
> snitch of honey

1. Using a food processor, blend carrots, almonds and dates into cake batter. Dump into a large mixing bowl.

2. Process currants, walnuts, coconut, vanilla, cinnamon and psyllium and add to the mixing bowl.

3. Squeeze lemon and mix in a tiny bit of honey.

4. Press batter firmly into cake pan and pour honey lemon mixture evenly over the top.

5. Refrigerate about one hour.

Option:
You can add **carob chips** to the batter if you like!

Carrot Cake Icing

> 1½ cup pitted medjool or honey dates, soaked in warm water for an hour and then drained
> 1 cup pine nuts, soaked for 20 minutes
> 1 tsp. lemon zest
> 2 T. fresh lemon juice
> 1½ tsp. vanilla

6. Blend all in a blender or food processor using the "S" blade. Use a little bit of carrot juice or water to thin if necessary.

7. Refrigerate one hour prior to icing the cake.

8. Garnish with finely chopped walnuts. Decorating the plate with flowers adds a nice touch.

Happy Birthday or whatever!

Raw Fruit Tart   ℝ

RawSome Kid Recipe!

Crust

> leftover pulp from *Almond Milk* (see *Breakfasts & Beverages*), or soak 1½ cups almonds over night. Drain and evenly grind nuts in food processor.
> 3/4 cup chopped, pitted medjool dates
> 1 T. raw almond butter
> 1 tsp. vanilla
> ½ tsp. cinnamon
> a few drops of water or almond milk, if necessary to create the right crust consistency

1. Process into a nice sturdy mix and immediately press into pie pan.

Filling

> 1 cup cashews, soaked overnight
> ½ cup or slightly more fresh squeezed orange juice
> 4 or 5 pitted dates
> couple of drops of almond extract

2. Whip up in food processor and spread on crust.

3. Top with your favorite sliced fruits. Slice in circles and arrange in patterns that please the eye!
    Get creative!

Option:
Dust with shredded **coconut**!

See photo of recipe on first page of this section.

Raw Oatmeal Cookies   ℝ

NOTE: dehydrator needed

> ¼ cup applesauce
> ¼–½ cup honey
> ¼ cup walnuts
> ½ cup shredded coconut
> 1 cup rolled oatmeal
> 1 cup currants

Process all ingredients. Shape one heaping T. of batter at a time into cookies and arrange on teflex sheet. Dehydrate for four hours.

Raw Pecan Pie R

(Inspired by Hallelujah Acres Food Show *Video)*

Crust

> 2 sliced bananas
> 1 papaya, sliced in thin long strips
> 1 ripe mango, sliced thin and long

1. Arrange sliced papaya and mango strips along the bottom of a glass pie pan.

2. Slice bananas into circles and place on the wall of the pie pan to form the outer crust.

3. Fill in any gaps on the bottom of the "crust" with any leftover sliced bananas.

Filling

> 12 pitted dates, soaked overnight
> 3/4 cup date-soak water
> 1 cup pecans, soaked overnight and drained
> 1 1/2 tsps. vanilla
> 1/4 tsp. nutmeg

4. Mix all ingredients into a thick paste in the food processor. Spoon over sliced-fruit crust.

Glazed Nut Topping

> 1 cup pecans
> 3 T. honey

5. Put above ingredients into container with tight lid and shake until pecans are coated.

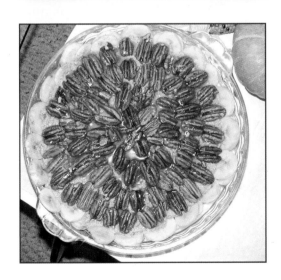

6 Arrange glazed pecans as shown in photo: place pecans around the edges and make circular patterns, filling the top of the pie. Keep placing circles inside of circles until you end up with one or two pecans in the very center of the pie.

Bonobo's Coconut Date Macaroons ℞

(This recipes comes from a fabulous raw restaurant called Bonobo's - 18 East 23rd St, New York)

1. In food processor, mix equal parts of:

    shredded mature coconut meat
    honey dates (or any live dates blended with coconut water until slightly runny)

2. Once you have a firm yet gooey mixture, shape into balls. You can use a small ice cream scoop to form the balls.

3. Drop macaroons onto dehydrator tray which has been wiped with a little raw coconut oil. No need to use the teflex sheets.

4. Dehydrate at about 105-110 degrees until you get the chewiness or crunchiness you like. The drier the macaroons the longer they will last. Keep refrigerated.

Option:

Add organic dried shredded coconut found in the bulk bins at health food stores, if the meat from the fresh young coconut is thin and mushy (as opposed to thick and meaty).

Raw Almond Joy Balls ℞

Using the leftover pulp from making a single recipe of **Almond Milk**, you can make a delicious "candy" that makes a great snack or treat in your child's lunchbox!

1. In food processor, mix almond pulp with:

    1/2 to 3/4 cup raw almond butter
    pulp from Almond Milk (see Breakfasts & Beverages)
    1/2 cup raisins or currants
    5 pitted dates soaked for 30 min. (or cut-up date pieces from date logs)
    1–3 T. honey, agave, or maple syrup
    1 tsp. cinnamon
    1 tsp. vanilla

2. Roll dough into 1 to 1 1/2-inch balls and divide balls into thirds.

3. Cover bottom of large plate with **shredded coconut**. Cover bottom of second plate with **carob powder**.

4. In a processor or coffee grinder, finely grind macadamia **nuts**.

6. Cover bottom of a third plate with the mac nuts. Roll each third of the balls in one of the three coatings. Enjoy!

Option:

Add **chopped nuts** of your choice or try **carob chips**! When you have a consistency that sticks together, roll into small balls. (The key is almond butter and honey for sticking power, so add more if need be!)

Brownies with Raspberry Fudge Icing ℝ

NOTE: dehydrator needed

(My version of an original recipe by Rose Lee Calabro)

> 2 cups walnuts, soaked 2–4 hours
> 1 cup pecans, soaked 2–4 hours
> 1 cup pine nuts, soaked 2 hours
> 1 cup pitted medjool dates at room temperature
> ½ ripe avocado
> ¼–½ cup maple syrup (depending on how sweet you like it)
> 2 tsp. vanilla
> pinch of salt

1. Mix pecans, pine nuts and dates together in processor.

2. Add avocado, carob, vanilla, maple syrup and pinch of salt. Mix well.

3. Add the walnuts and process into firm dough.

4. Scoop up ¼ cup of dough at a time and form into a rectangular-shaped brownie no more than ½-inch thick.

5. Place on dehydrator tray using a teflex sheet. Dehydrate four to five hours at 105°.

6. Turn brownies over and remove the teflex sheet. Dehydrate another six hours.

Icing

> ½ cup fresh raspberries
> ¼ cup maple syrup
> 2 tsp. vanilla
> ¼ cup plus 1 tsp. carob powder

7. Using the "S" blade, whirl the raspberries, maple syrup and vanilla together. Add carob slowly and mix well.

8. Refrigerate for a half hour.

9. Using a spreading spatula ice the brownies. Enjoy with a glass of fresh **Almond Milk** (*see Breakfasts & Beverages*).

Banana Berry Swirl ℝ

> 2 cups frozen blueberries
> 2 large frozen bananas

1. Peel and break bananas into thirds.

2. Place banana pieces into gallon zip lock bag and freeze.

3. Press the bananas through a juicer using the blank plate. Let the frozen bananas swirl into a dish.

4. Now repeat the process using blueberries, allowing them to swirl next to the banana ice cream.

Option: Try using **blackberries** or **strawberries** instead of blueberries.

Banana Coconut Date Ice Cream ℞

3 young coconuts
4 pitted medjool dates at room temperature
½ frozen banana

1. Hack open three young coconuts. *(See photos on the back of the book on how to open. Notice that I use the rear edge of a butcher knife to create the right stroke to penetrate the outer shell)*

2. Scrape out the meat of all three coconuts and place in a blender.

3. Use the coconut water from one coconut. Save the water from the other two to drink at another time.

4. Add the four dates to the blender.

5. Whirl on highest setting until you have a nice thick shake.

6. Place in ice cube trays and freeze overnight.

7. The next day, or once the coconut milk is frozen, repeat steps 1–5. You will be using this fresh, unfrozen batch of coconut-date milk with the frozen coconut milk.

8. Place frozen coconut-date milk in food processor with frozen banana and pulse to break it down.

9. Now slowly pour in some fresh coconut-date milk and turn processor on. Watch as it whirls and slowly add more milk until you get a nice creamy ice cream texture.

10. Add more frozen bananas or room-temperature dates for a sweeter taste.

Option:
Can add **shredded coconut**.

Coconut Vanilla Bean Ice Cream ℞

1 batch of *Almond Milk,* made using the water from young coconuts
** instead of water**
2 fresh whole vanilla beans
1 banana peeled, broken into thirds and frozen

1. Make a batch of *Fresh Almond Milk* (See recipe under Breakfast and Beverages) and substitute the water from fresh young coconuts instead of plain water.

2. Grate two vanilla beans into the milk and stir until blended.

3. Pour the milk into ice cube trays and freeze.

4. Press the ice cubes through a juicer using the blank plate.

5. Transfer the frozen coconut and vanilla bean milk into a processor. Using the "S" blade, mix the frozen milk with one or two pieces of frozen banana. The banana will make it creamy. Don't use too much banana, as that will tend to dominate the flavor.

Option:
Serve with **fresh peaches** and **blackberries** for a delicious treat! You can also top with **chopped almonds** or **walnuts**.

Strawberry, Piña Colada Popsicles R

> 16 oz. of pineapple-coconut juice
> 1 banana
> 1 cup fresh strawberries
> 1 cup shredded coconut

1. Blend all ingredients in blender.

2. Pour into popsicle molds (best to get two sets of six) and freeze. Great on a hot summer afternoon!

Banana Ice Cream with Raspberry Sauce R

> 2–4 large bananas, peeled, broken into thirds and frozen
> ½ cup fresh raspberries
> 2 T. maple syrup
> 1 tsp. water
> 1 T. almond milk
> 1 tsp. organic coconut oil

1. Press the bananas through a juicer using the blank plate to make banana ice cream.

2. To make the sauce, mix all other ingredients in food processor and pour on top of banana ice cream.

Orange Zest Freezer Fudge R

RawSome Kid Recipe!

> 3/4 cups pine nuts, soaked ½ hour
> 1 cup pecans, soaked with ½ cup pitted dates for half hour
> 3/4 cups walnuts, soaked with ½ cup pitted dates for half hour
> ½ cup walnuts, soaked alone for ½ hour
> 5 T. carob powder
> ¼ cup maple syrup
> 2 tsp. vanilla
> ½–1 tsp. orange zest (depending on your taste)

1. Drain all nuts and dates, keeping the additional ½ cup walnuts separate from everything else. Chop these walnuts into small bits and set aside to use on the top at the end.

2. Process all other nuts and dates through a juicer using the blank plate (for a better consistency) or in a food processor using the "S" blade.

3. Add carob, maple syrup, vanilla and orange zest. Spread in 6 x 10 rectangular glass pan.

4. Sprinkle the reserved walnuts on top.

5. Score into even squares.

6. Cover and freeze.

Clever Carob Pudding ℞

(Original recipe by Pam Masters)

> 2 T. carob powder
> 1 cup water
> 1 tsp. vanilla
> 1/4 tsp. cinnamon
> 10 soaked and pitted dates
> 1 avocado
> 4 sliced strawberries

1. In a food processor, combine all ingredients except for the strawberries, dates and avocado.

2. While processor is running, slowly add dates and avocado until smooth.

3. Alternate layers of strawberries with pudding in long-stemmed glasses and top with sliced berries.

Note:
Adding more water will turn this from pudding into a sauce you can pour over **Banana Ice Cream** (see recipe this section) or whatever!

Banana Cream Parfait ℞

RawSome Kid Recipe!

Large martini glasses or any other festive glass work well for this.

> 1/2–1 cup *Good Morning Granola* (see *Breakfasts & Beverages*)
> 1 large very ripe banana
> 2 T. *Almond Milk* (see *Breakfasts & Beverages*)
> 1/2 tsp. vanilla
> fresh peach slices
> fresh blackberries

1. Blend the banana together with the almond milk and vanilla until creamy.

2. Start with a layer of granola on the bottom of the glass.

3. Spoon some banana cream over the granola.

4. Add some blackberries and peaches, then begin again with the granola followed by the banana cream.

5. Lean sliced peaches over the edge of the glass, similar to how shrimp cocktails are served. Fill in the top with blueberries.

Razzle Dazzle Lime Parfait R

   2 avocados
   juice from 2 limes
   1 – 2 T. agave

1   Whip the above ingredients in food processor until light and creamy.

2.   Fill a tall parfait glass one-fourth full with this vibrant green cream.

   1 package frozen organic raspberries (from Trader Joe's)
   ¼ cup fresh young coconut meat
   ¼ – ½ cup coconut water
   2 T. agave

3.   Blend above four ingredients and make a thin raspberry red layer over the green cream.

   meat from two young coconuts
   ½ – 1 cup coconut water
   2 – 4 pitted room temperature dates

4.   Whip these three ingredients in processor, and then make a thin layer over the raspberry layer.

5.   Finish filling the parfait glass with another layer of raspberry sauce and a final topping of coconut cream. **Or...** make layers in any order or thickness that pleases your individual palate! Garnish with **chopped nuts** or slice **kiwis** and place them around the rim. This recipe was inspired from a dessert I had at the fabulous Candle 79, at 154 East 79th Street in my favorite city... New York!

Granola Parfait S

RawSome Kid Recipe!

   ½–1 cup *Good Morning Granola* (see *Breakfasts*)
   fresh blueberries
   vanilla goat yogurt

Using a wide mouth glass or wine glass, make several layers using the above ingredients. This is a favorite after school snack at our house.

Mango Madness Ice Cream S

RawSome Kid Recipe!

   ½ package frozen mangos from Trader Joe's (or freeze cut-up pieces of 2 large mangos)
   ¼ vanilla goat yogurt or ⅓ cup almond milk
   1 large frozen banana

1.   Place ingredients in processor and use pulse button to chunk down the mango and banana pieces.

2.   Slowly drizzle in more almond milk or yogurt while processor continues to whirl.

3.   Watch closely so you don't water it down too much. For thicker ice cream use more mangos, or to thin use more yogurt or almond milk!

RawSome Apple Crisp 🅢

RawSome Kid Recipe!

> 8–10 cooking apples
> juice of 1 lemon
> 1/2 cup orange juice
> 2 cups raw oats
> 3/4 cup whole wheat flour
> 1/2 cup butter
> 1/3 cup honey
> 1 tsp. cinnamon
> 1 tsp. vanilla
> 1/2 currants

1. Peel apples and drizzle with lemon juice.

2. Spread half in pan.

3. Melt butter and honey together.

4. Combine with the oats, flour, cinnamon, currants and vanilla.

5. Crumble half of this mixture on first layer of apples.

6. Repeat a second layer with the rest of the apples and topping.

7. Pour the orange juice over the top.

8. Bake at 375° for 40–45 minutes. Once apples are crispy and soft, pull out of oven and serve.

9. Create a fun dessert bar by setting out the following options of raw toppings to go with the warmed apple crisp. This way you get some raw food in with the cooked. Thus, *RawSome Apple Crisp!*

> chopped walnuts
> finely chopped macadamia nuts
> vanilla goat yogurt
> homemade *Banana Ice Cream* (see recipe this section)
> sunflower seeds
> almond milk (to pour over crisp)
> fresh berries
> fresh peach slices

Strawberry Frozen Yogurt S

RawSome Kid Recipe!

> **2 cups frozen berries**
> **1 cup strawberry goat yogurt (made by Redwood Hill Farms)**
> **2–3 T. agave or honey**

Blend all ingredients using the "S" blade in the processor. For thicker ice cream use more berries, or to thin use more yogurt or almond milk!

Wholly Oatmeal Cookies S

RawSome Kid Recipe!

Mix together:

> **3 bananas**
> **1/3 cup applesauce or melted butter**
> **1 cup raisins or pitted dates**
> **1 tsp. vanilla**

Once thoroughly mixed add:

> **2 cups raw oats**
> **1/2 cup chopped nuts**

Bake at 350° for five or 10 minutes

Serve with a nice glass of homemade almond milk.

Macro Bars S

RawSome Kid Recipe!

> **1/2 cup melted organic butter**
> **1/2 cup agave or honey (or kids love it with maple syrup)**
> **1 1/4 cup whole wheat pastry flour**
> **1/2 cup rolled oats**
> **1/2 cup millet, ground in processor or coffee grinder**
> **1 tsp. cinnamon**
> **1 cup prunes, soaked in enough warm purified water to cover prunes for 1 hour**

1. Drain prunes, saving soak water.
2. Combine all ingredients except for prunes. If too dry, slowly add prune juice soak water.
3. Spread dough on cookie sheet. Keep hands moist so it doesn't stick.
4. Process prunes with enough soak water to make into a firm but spreadable icing.
5. Spread prune topping on batter and bake 25 minutes at 350°. Cut into squares and enjoy.

Apple & Pumpkin Harvest Pie S

Top Layer

Preheat oven to 425°.

> 1 large sugar pumpkin (or a 15 oz. can of organic pumpkin, which will speed up the process of this delicious pie)
> 2 eggs (or 4 egg whites lightly beaten)
> 1 cup almond milk
> ½ cup agave or maple syrup
> 3 tsp. pumpkin pie spice
> ½ tsp. salt
> 1 apple cut in quarters, sliced very thin
> A dozen or so pecans

1. If using fresh pumpkin, follow steps below. If using canned pumpkin, go to Step 5.
2. Cut open pumpkin and scrape out the seeds and stringy bits.
3. Slice into pieces and steam or bake until soft.
4. Remove the outer skin and mash the pumpkin meat in food processor.
5. Measure out the equivalent of a 15 oz can of pumpkin.
6. Mix all ingredients except apples together in food processor.
7. Grease up a pie pan with either organic butter or coconut oil.
8. Pour ingredients into pie pan and bake at 425° for 15 minutes, then reduce temperature to 350°.
9. After 20 minutes, check to see if mixture is firm enough to support the weight of thinly-sliced apples. When it is, place the apple slices on top of the pumpkin and continue baking for another 20–30 minutes, or until the pumpkin is firm.

Crust

> 2 cups *Honey 'N Nuts Munchie Mix* (see recipe in *Honorable Hors d'Oeuvres...*), or any combo of nuts you like that have been soaked for at least 2 hours (soak almonds for at least 6 hours) then rinsed and drained
> 8 pitted dates at room temperature
> 1 T. honey

10. While the pumpkin is baking, mix all ingredients in the processor and then press into a pie plate. Make sure to build crust all the way up the side walls.

recipe continues next page

Apple & Pumpkin Harvest Pie ~ *continued*

Apple Layer

> **4–5 large apples (I like Fuji, but use your favorite or blend a few different ones)**
> **1 tsp. cinnamon**
> **1 tsp. vanilla**

11. Peel and core the apples.

12. Process into applesauce. For a chunkier sauce use the pulse button. I prefer to make it smooth.

13. Spoon the fresh, raw applesauce on top of the crust.

14. Once the pumpkin filling has cooled, remove the thin apple slices and set aside.

15. Spoon the pumpkin filling on top of the applesauce layer. Now use your fingers to spread the pumpkin evenly to all edges and to make a consistent texture.

16. Decorate the top with the thinly sliced apples and pecans anyway you wish.

Banana Flaxseed Bread *S*

> **½ cup agave or honey**
> **½ cup vanilla goat yogurt**
> **1 egg**
> **¼ cup applesauce**
> **1 cup whole wheat flour**
> **¾ cup flaxseed, ground in coffee grinder**
> **1 tsp. baking powder**
> **1 tsp. baking soda**
> **pinch of salt**
> **1 cup very ripe bananas, puréed**

1. Preheat oven to 350° and butter up an 4 x 8 loaf pan.

2. In a large bowl, mix first four ingredients.

3. In a medium bowl combine everything else except bananas.

4. Whisk wet ingredients together and combine with dry ingredients.

5. Stir just until blended, taking care not to over-mix.

6. Fold in bananas and stir just enough to mix.

7. Bake 40–50 minutes. Let cool before cutting.

Serve with a nice cup of herbal tea!

Pumpkin Pie Ice Cream S

> 1 can 15 oz. organic pumpkin
> 1 cup almond milk or better yet, 1 cup *Whipped Coconut Dream Cream*
>   (see steps 2-4 next page)
> 1/3–1/2 cup maple syrup or agave
> 2 tsp. pumpkin pie spice
> 1 vanilla bean grated

1. Mix all ingredients in food processor and freeze in ice cube tray.

2. Put frozen pumpkin mixture in processor with a small piece of frozen banana.

3. Add vanilla goat yogurt or almond milk slowly while processor is turning until desired ice cream consistency is reached.

Yum yum... happy holiday times!

Special Treat Cake S

RawSome Kid Recipe!

> 1 cup maple syrup
> 1 diced apple
> 1/2 cup vanilla goat yogurt
> 1/4 cup melted organic butter
> 2 T. applesauce
> 1 tsp. vanilla
> 1 tsp. salt
> 2 egg yolks
> 3/4 cup ground hazelnuts (mac nuts or walnuts are ok, too!)
> 1 1/2 cups whole wheat pastry flour
> 1 1/2 tsp. baking soda
> 3 egg whites

1. Mix the first eight ingredients.

2. Then mix together everything else except for egg whites.

3. Mix these two together.

4. Beat the egg whites and fold them in.

5. Grease and flour a 10-inch round cake tin and bake at 350° for 40 minutes.

Option:
You can slice some **apples** very thin and float on top of the cake once it has baked and set up for a while (check after the first 20–30 minutes of baking). Place back in the oven and finish baking.

Baked Pears &
Fresh Whipped Coconut Dream Cream   *S*

assortment of pears (2 per person)
2 coconuts
4–6 pitted, room-temperature medjool dates
Honey 'N Nuts Munchie Mix **(see** *Honorable Hors d'Oeuvres…***)**

1. Wash pears and bake at 375° with skins intact on a Pyrex dish until very soft and bubbly.

2. Meanwhile, open 2 coconuts, scrape out all the meat and place into a blender.

3. Add only half the water from one coconut, a little liquid at a time.

4. Use 4–6 dates and whip everything together vigorously in blender. Add more coconut water if need be (in small amounts), until you get a nice creamy, whipped consistency.

5. Spoon out the buttery soft meat of the pears and discard the skins.

6. Pour the coconut cream over piping hot pears.

7. Top with *Honey 'N Nuts Munchie Mix*.

So yum! Great for Christmas Eve!

RawSome Resources

Planning
Meals Ahead, Glossary
of Ingredients

&

Resources for
Tools & Products

RawSome Resources

Planning Meals Ahead

I would like to help you make meal planning and thinking ahead a little easier, so I will attempt to lay out ideas to help you be more organized. I will give you examples from my typical weekly meals and go through each meal with some suggestions.

First, if you ever feel that you are not getting enough protein in any meal, then a simple solution is to add 1 tsp. of **Pure Planet plain** or **carob mint spirulina** to a smoothie. Another form of supplemental spirulina comes in easy-to-digest tablets which can be chewed, to increase absorption, or swallowed with water if you can't handle the taste. The tablets are very convenient—they can be carried in your pocket whether you are working, hiking or wherever you may be. I use the powder in my morning smoothie, and throughout the day I chew on the tablets.

Breakfast

Recipes that require prior prep:

1. *Almond Milk* – soak almonds in water the night before

2. Freeze an assortment of **berries and bananas** (place berries and bananas in separate freezer bags) to always have on hand for various smoothies. When freezing bananas, be sure to remove the skins and break each banana into three pieces.

3. *New Natives Breakfast Jump Start* – make it easy by doing these two steps before going to bed:

   a Soak apricots, raisins, and cinnamon in apple juice overnight.

   b. In a separate jar, soak sunflower, flax and pumpkin seeds in water. Drain and rinse after one hour. Let sprout overnight.

4 *RawSome Oatmeal* – soak overnight, one cup per serving of raw oats in enough water to cover. In the morning, drain and place in food processor with ½ tsp. cinnamon, two or three pitted dates, and process. Pour into a bowl and add some almond milk. Top with slivered almonds and mixed berries.

Robyn's morning breakfast:

Upon arising, I have 1 tsp. of Just Barley in eight ounces of water. Anywhere from half an hour to an hour later I make the following smoothie:

8 oz. almond milk

1 T. Twinlab's Yeast Plus/brewer's yeast

¼ cup flaxseeds

1 tsp. carob mint spirulina

½ banana

Grind flaxseeds in grinder. Mix all ingredients in a blender. This smoothie fills me with wonderful nutrition and takes me all the way through a very active morning until lunchtime.

Lunch

Recipes that require prior prep:

1. Make *Cashew Pate* the night before to let flavors blend and then use as *Santa Cruz Solar Tacos* the next day for lunch.

2. Make *Tabbouleh* the night before and take in a container to lunch. This lasts in the refrigerator for three days.

3. For *Sandra's Brilliantly Beyond Tuna Salad,* soak nuts and seeds for 3 hours and let drain for eight hours (or overnight).

Typical lunches that I enjoy:

For me, lunch is usually a large salad, and I have several salad dressings made up ahead. I always have a batch of *Home Base Salad Dressing* on hand ready to go for dressing or for many other recipes such as stir fries, etc. Plan to make a batch whenever you have some time and store it in a large Mason jar. It will keep for several weeks in the fridge.

Every once in awhile, or for those transitioning, you may want to add organic feta cheese or a hard-boiled egg, depending on whether you are vegan or not. If I have prepped the night before, then I will add a scoop of *Sandra's Brilliantly Beyond Tuna Salad.*

Another lunch choice for me is pita pockets stuffed with avocados or *Gorgeous Guacamole.* If I eat any type of sandwich, I always fill them to overflowing with sunflower sprouts, fresh tomatoes, and grated carrots. I like to use sheets of nori, lettuce, or napa cabbage leaves in place of bread to create delicious avocado and veggie sandwiches.

Afternoon Snack:

In the afternoon around 3pm, I enjoy a green drink of either wheatgrass or barley grass and about a half hour later an apple.

Dinner

The main event at most dinners at our house is SALAD!

Recipes that require prior prep:

When life is busy and time is short, meals get very simple and that is a good thing! When you have time, it is best to prepare salsa and beans ahead of time. Then during the week when life is too hurried, this makes wonderful fast meals.

You can also make *RawSome Pesto Sauce* or *Raw Marinara Sauce* ahead and use on baked potatoes or zucchini pasta the next day.

Soups and stews always taste better the next day as flavors blend. When I am organized I prefer to use a crock pot. It is great to pop things in the pot in the morning and have it warm and ready to go by dinnertime. Crock pots work well for stews like *Rawsome Ratatouille.*

Here are some typical dinners at our house when life is busy:

Monday Night:

Salad with *Raw Cabbage Burritos* or bean burritos and salsa

Tuesday Night:

Salad bar with either baked potatoes with *RawSome Pesto Sauce* or baked yams, or *Robyn's Roast Potato Medley*

Wednesday Night:

Salad with veggie burgers

Thursday Night:

Salad with *Brown Rice and Veggies with Purple Confetti*

Friday Night:

Raw Spinach Lasagna with Cashew Ricotta with salad (for vegans) or Salad with steamed salmon and fresh asparagus or fish tacos with Mango Tango Salsa (for those transitioning or non vegan)

Saturday Night:

Salad with a hearty soup or stew, often with whole grain bread and butter or cornbread

Sunday Night:

Salad with *Lovely Lentil, Millet & Nut Loaf, Wholly Gravy* and steamed veggies

Things to always have on hand prepped:

1. *Home Base Dressing*
2. two or three salad dressings
3. frozen berries, frozen mangos, frozen bananas
4. frozen veggie burgers and buns
5. feta cheese (non vegans/those transitioning)
6. hard boiled eggs (non vegans/those transitioning)

Fit for Company... Four All-Raw Dinner Menus

When your company first arrives, serve them either coconut water from a fresh young coconut or an *Amé Wineless Cooler* (see *Breakfasts & Beverages*).

Fresh young coconuts come wrapped in plastic and are sold in Asian markets and some health food and gourmet stores. These coconuts are white in appearance on the outside and must be hacked open in order to find the nut with its delicious water and fresh meat contained within. It is best to store the coconuts in the refrigerator until you are ready to serve them.

See the photos to the left, which demonstrate the process described below. Please be very careful!

In order to open your coconut, use a rectangular butcher knife. Using the corner of the blade that is closest to the handle, hack a hexagon in the top of the coconut. This takes practice and a steady hand. Once you have hacked a hexagon around the top, you can use your hands to peel the top back. Insert a straw and serve or pour into a chilled glass. Using the back of a spoon loosen the meat away from the shell of the coconut. The meat can be eaten just as is or turned into all kinds of wonderful treats ranging from mock "noodles" to puddings and pie fillings.

Amé Wineless Coolers, served with fresh fruit floating in the glass, make a wonderful wine substitute. This provides a nice refreshing sparkle to set a lovely tone for the dinner.

Dinner Menu #1

Thai Appetizer
Cream of Tomato Soup
Veggie Stir Un-fry with Ginger Yum Yum Sauce
Mango Madness Ice Cream

Dinner Menu #2

Heirloom Tomatoes with Basil and Young Coconut
Zucchini Pasta w/Pesto and Marinara Sauce—use zucchinis for one half of the platter and top with *Marinara Sauce,* and yellow zucchinis topped with *RawSome Pesto Sauce* for the other half of the platter.
Robyn's Roast Potato Medley
Green Salad with your choice of ingredients, with *Home Base Sauce*
RawSome Apricot & Peach Cobbler and/or *Coconut Vanilla Bean Ice Cream*

Dinner Menu #3

Sweet Corn Crackers with *Fernando's Fabulous Mango Tango Salsa*
Cabbage Burritos
Summer Splendor Salad
Freezer Fudge or *Raw Fruit Tart*

Dinner Menu #4

Veggies and *Mock Ranch Dip* or *Cashew Pate* with *Italian Flax Crackers*
Raw Spinach Lasagna with Cashew Ricotta
Spa Salad

Apple Juice Slushies

Banana Almond Milk Shakes

Banana Cream Parfait

Banana Flaxseed Bread

Coconut Date Shake

Fresh Apple Pear Juice
  (*Miss Molly's favorite juice*)

Freezer Fudge

Fruit Salad

Granola Parfaits

Honey 'N Nuts Munchie Mix

Macro Bars

Mango Madness Ice Cream

Molly's Mango Lasse

Orange Zest Freezer Fudge

Raw Almond Joy Balls

Raw Oatmeal Cookies

Mock Ranch Dressing /dip with veggies

Smoothies

Strawberry Frozen Yogurt

Strawberry Pina Colada Popsicles

Wholly Oatmeal Cookies

Yumlishious Almond Protein Drink

Clever Carob Pudding or *Brownies with Raspberry Fudge Icing*

Snacks

Great After-school Snacks and Grazing Foods for Play Dates

Bowls of grazing foods like: nuts and seeds, strawberries, really sweet cherry tomatoes, grapes, fresh blueberries or sliced oranges, kiwis and apples. These foods can be magically set out on counters and replenished by unknown silent little helper elves when the kids aren't looking! Set these foods out and invite the kids to help themselves whenever they want.

Also set out a pitcher of lemon water and cups and encourage the kids to help themselves whenever they are thirsty.

Rawsome Holiday Menu

Hors d'Oeuvres

Amé Wineless Coolers for the adults and Party Punch for the kids, or:

Fresh Coconut Water Cocktails

Thai Appetizer

Cashew Pate served in mini pumpkins with Sundried Tomato Flaxseed Crackers and Flax To The Max Crackers

Rawsome Hummus with assorted veggies

Main Course

Festive Winter Salad

Christmas Quinoa Salad

Lovely Lentil, Millet & Nut Loaf with Garlic Mashed Cauliflower and Wholly Gravy

Yum Yum Yam Salad

Broccoli and Cranberry Salad

Wonderful Waldorf Salad with Almonnaise

Rawsome Dessert

Tray with assortment of:

Raw Almond Joy Balls

Macro Bars

Apple and Pumpkin Harvest Pie

Raw Pecan Pie

Pumpkin Pie Ice Cream

This menu makes for a wonderful party! Find a group of friends to celebrate life with and divide up the items. Enjoy a wonderful special feast!

Pointers:

1. You need to plan ahead for the hummus. Begin soaking garbanzos 3 days prior to event.
2. It is best to make cashew pate the day before so that the flavors can blend.
3. You can make the following items the night before if you want to give yourself time the day of your event:

Yum Yum Yam Salad, Broccoli and Cranberry Salad, Raw Almond Joy Balls, Macro Bars and Rawsome Hummus (which always tastes better served chilled, letting the flavors blend overnight).

Transitioning a Step at a Time

This list is intended to support you in taking easy, "doable" steps toward living a healthier, more vibrant life. Think of it as a check list, or for some, a *reality* check list! From time to time you can go back and look over the list and fine tune. Sometimes it's nice just to pick one thing and really focus on that one thing for the coming week. Then when you think you have that integrated into your lifestyle add one more thing from the list. You can do these things in any order you choose. Have fun with this. Make it an adventure (not a should or have-to thing)!

1. **Use the "Replace The Old and Embrace The New list"** under *Shifting To Whole Foods* to constantly keep upgrading. Place pencil checks on the list for the items that you have upgraded.

2. **Upgrade kitchen tools** beginning with glass jars. Begin to transfer all stored food items into glass jars. If you can't afford to buy new Mason Jars then use recycled jars. Old juice bottles work well for storing grains and legumes. Old jam jars work well for spices and teas. Also make sure you are working with sharp knives.

3. **Make sure you are drinking adequate amounts of water.** Try adding fresh lemon juice into your water for added benefits.

4. **Add a green drink** like wheatgrass or spirulina into your daily routine.

5. **Now, try to consistently drink a green drink once in the morning and once in the afternoon.**

6. **Eat one piece of fruit a day.**

7. **Add at least one piece of fruit, two green drinks and one salad a day.** Try to do that for three days in the upcoming week.

8. **In addition to the above, add one more fruit.** Now attempt to consume two fruits, two green drinks and one salad per day for three out of seven days. Continue this routine but increase the number of days of the week until it becomes a daily habit.

9. **Reduce your caffeine consumption by one third.** Next take it down to two thirds. Now try skipping a day and then gradually put more and more distance between consumption until it fades away! It can be helpful to replace caffeine with vital green drinks.

10. **Cut way back on sugar.** Start replacing sugar with honey, agave, dates or stevia.

11. **Replace cow's milk with almond milk.** Switch cow cheese and yogurt over to goat.

12. **Daily, add in more raw foods.** Try soaking nuts and seeds and snacking on them.

13. **Start or recommit to juicing.** If you don't have a juicer, go to a juice bar.

14. **Try making one new healthy recipe a week.** Plan ahead, shop ahead.

15. **Go to the Farmers Market and buy one new thing** you have never tried, or hardly ever get.

16. **Invite friends over and make them something all raw.** It can be a snack instead of a whole meal at first! Share what you are learning with others.

17. **Get in three or more days of exercise.**

Enjoy the process! Eat well and be well! Cheers!

Tips for Healthy Traveling

Whether I'm getting ready to jet off or hit the highway I always go prepared. Just a few items can transform your travels. A few days before I leave, I try to make sure to eat well, do my green drinks (barley grass, kamut, or spirulina) at least twice a day, drink plenty of water and get all rested up. Starting the journey off on the right foot helps you go a lot further down the road.

The essential travel kit check list:

✓ Barley grass powder
✓ Carob mint spirulina tabs made by Pure Planet
✓ Carob mint spirulina powder
✓ Twin Lab Yeast Plus powder
✓ Pro Fiber E.F.A. – a must have to keep the bowels moving while on the road!
✓ Glass jar with a lid or plastic shake container to whip up a morning smoothie
✓ Igloo lunch box cooler
✓ Frozen slushie
✓ Ranch dressing/dip with sliced red and orange bell peppers, carrots sticks, cucumbers and celery
✓ Homemade salad dressing
✓ Purified water in a stainless steel thermos
✓ Calms Forté; homeopathic remedy made by Hylands to help you sleep with no side effects
✓ 1 carton of almond milk made by Pacific
✓ Lavender oil*
✓ Peppermint oil*
✓ Thieves oil*
✓ Thieves wipes or spray*
✓ Oregano oil*
✓ Lemon oil*
✓ Purification oil*
✓ Dentarome Plus with Thieves toothpaste*
✓ Diffuser - to help combat airborne germs and cleanse and purify the air in places like hotels

Igloo makes a wonderful lunch-size cooler which is perfect for airplane travel. Buy guacamole in the freezer section of Trader Joe's if you have one of their stores near you, or make up a batch and freeze. Also freeze juice (like you would to make Slushies in the *Breakfasts & Beverages* chapter) or water in a plastic bottle. Use the guacamole, frozen juice or water to keep items in your cooler cold. When the guacamole and juice or water thaw, you can use them until you get settled at your destination. Fill your cooler with small containers of salad dressings that you can use at restaurants, and therefore avoid dressings that have MSG and other harmful ingredients. Make room in the cooler for the Ranch dressing and fresh veggies

* For more information regarding the oils see next section: Essential Oils For Home and Travel

to munch on while you are on the road or in the air. The fresh veggies can also be used to eat with the thawed guacamole.

For breakfast on the road I place 1 heaping tsp. spirulina powder, 2 tsp. Brewer's Yeast powder, and 1 heaping tsp. Pro Fiber E.F.A. in almond milk and shake it up in a jar or plastic shaker bottle. This gives me the nutrients I need to get my days away from home off to a good balanced nutritious start! If I know I will have access to a blender I will bring a banana to add to the mix. The banana helps sweeten the blend and smooth out the texture.

Essential Oils for Home and Travel

Essential oils have been used in various cultures for thousands of years as incense, perfumes and cosmetics, in culinary application and most importantly as medicine. These subtle, highly complex liquids are distilled from plants, shrubs, flowers, trees, roots, bushes and seeds.

Both frankincense and myrrh, as well as many other oils referred to in the Bible,* contain powerful healing agents. There are several important reasons the baby Jesus was given gifts of frankincense and myrrh. Herbs of this caliber were considered amongst the treasures of the earth. According to *The Illustrated Encyclopedia of Essential Oils* by Julia Lawless, frankincense is known to have the following actions: anti-inflammatory, antiseptic, astringent, digestive, diuretic, expectorant and sedative. She also cites the actions of myrrh to include: anticatarrhal, anti-inflammatory, antimicrobial, antiphlogistic, antiseptic, astringent, expectorant, fungicidal, revitalizing, sedative and tonic.

I have been using essential oils both personally with my family and professionally with my massage clients and have seen some fantastic results for a wide range of issues and symptoms.

There are many companies worldwide involved in the aromatherapy industry today. As with the health food and supplement industry, it is wise to do your own research and find what works best in your own body. There are some contraindications for the safe use of essential oils, such as pregnancy, high blood pressure, and those with sensitive skin. Reactions can happen with essential oils similar to reactions that people experience with some foods, so doing a skin patch test initially is advisable.

Some essential oils that I have found to be extremely beneficial are made by a company called Young Living Essential Oils. They make some very interesting blends and there is one in particular that I will never again leave home without! It is called Thieves, as a result of research out of the English archives.

A group of fourteen thieves made history because they were able to avoid contracting the plague while robbing the bodies of the dead and dying. It was later found that their secret weapon of survival was a brilliant formula of herbs, spices and oils combined to provide ultimate protection against the deadly germs. When apprehended by the authorities, they exchanged their secret formula for less severe criminal punishment. According to *People's Desk Reference for Essential Oils,* compiled by Essential Science Publishing, this very blend has been tested at Weber State University and found to have a 99.96% kill rate against airborne bacteria. The combination of the oils used in this blend packs an arsenal of defense, waging war against germs in a mighty way. These collective oils are known to be highly successful in

such as galbanum, cinnamon, cassia, rosemary, hyssop and spikenard, all used for anointing and healing the sick.

thwarting off flu, colds, sinusitis, bronchitis, pneumonia and sore throats as well as staving off infections from cuts and open wounds. This historic potent mix contains oils of clove, lemon, cinnamon bark, eucalyptus and rosemary.

Here's a personal example. My husband and daughter flew home from LA just days before we were heading out on our last family vacation for the summer. It is very probable that they were vulnerable to something or other from that flight, as is often the case after flying these days. The night before we were leaving, as we were packing up the car to head out, my husband said his throat was sore. My daughter had already had that for a day and was heading into the land of goop. I got out my Thieves oil and diffused it in our bedrooms.

I am convinced that essential oils hold a very important key in unlocking the door to health, recovery, and maintaining wellness.

As I kissed my daughter good night I rubbed the oil on the bottom of her feet and a little bit on her chest. I did the same with my husband. Molly's entire cold lasted a day and a half! My husband was good to go in the morning and off we went down the highway. He never had any head cold symptoms. Things just went straight into a chest cough. On and off I would use the oils. He never missed a beat on our trip and enjoyed hiking, biking, boating and long days of driving with only a cough now and again as a reminder that he was not quite completely well.

We used the various oils constantly on that trip. Lavender and peppermint helped tremendously with a migraine. Oregano, along with Thieves, helped to ward off what they had so I never even got a touch of any symptoms. Peppermint oil was wonderful for cutting Molly's car sickness on long twisty roads. Lavender stopped the annoying itch of sunburn or bug bites. Overnight, frankincense cleared up a sore that up to that point, was taking forever to heal. Lemon oil in water helped to act as a diuretic on days when the heat made digits swell. The blend called Joy just added a nice sweetness and "upliftment" to the air when the time spent on the road began to ride us!

Young Living has a line of wonderful products that contain the Thieves oil blend. These are a "must have" on my travel list as well as the home list! Instead of reaching for the chemical (and often toxic) household cleaners and sprays to combat household airborne bacteria and germs, there is a great alternative! Now we can use Thieves Household Cleaner in the form of a spray or wipes. These products can be used anywhere you want to destroy germs and bacteria. Great to use at work, in public restrooms, on planes, trains, or in automobiles! They have even come up with a purse or briefcase size spray bottle perfect for travel. As if that isn't enough, they have thought of everything! The wonders of Thieves can also be found in throat lozenges as well as in an all-natural toothpaste called Dentarome Plus. What a great concept for toothpaste to include oils that are known to be antimicrobial.

I am in no way an expert about the use and benefits of essential oils, but I plan to learn as much as I can. From what I have already experienced, I am convinced that they hold a very important key in unlocking the door to health, recovery, and maintaining wellness.

I decided to become a distributor of these products because I am thrilled with the results I get. These products are quite expensive and have to be bought through a Network Marketing structure. Those two issues are definitely deterrents for some people and I can fully understand that, as those are typically concerns of mine as well. However, I learned that Young Living chose this approach to marketing as they believe it is important for the customers to receive proper education on the most effective use of the oils. Network Marketing provides a way to give one on one instruction. This approach also allows for group trainings on the benefits of, and the appropriate, safe application of all their products. As some put it, these oils are "the Rolls Royce of oils." Yes, they are more expensive, but once properly educated, many agree these oils hold their own in quality and results. If you are interested in finding out more about Young Living Oils or ordering, you can go to **www.youngliving.com** and type in my referral number, which is **717229**.

I encourage you to keep searching and educating yourself about the wonderful benefits of using quality therapeutic grade essential oils. I believe in the coming times there will be much more talk about the use of oils and their benefits (especially in a world where we are finding that antibiotics are not able to do what they once were able to do). Quality is very critical with essential oils. There is much to learn about the production—the importance of how the herbs are handled from the soil all the way to distillation and packaging. The point is not that I want you to order from me, but I want to encourage you to research and learn about the wonderful benefits of using high quality essential oils for most of your everyday needs. Just be sure that no matter what oil you use, they are of the purest and highest quality, grown organically in healthy soil. There are definitely other good companies out there as well as Young Living. Find what works!

Glossary of Ingredients

Agave: Nectar from the Blue Agave cactus native to Mexico. Tastes like honey and maple syrup combined, yet is superior as it measures lower on the glycemic index, hence is processed differently in the body. Works well for those with blood sugar issues. 100% Raw Organic Agave Nectar can be purchased ($16.95 for 16 fluid oz.) from Nature's First Law on their secure online superstore: **www.rawfood.com** or call toll-free 800-205-2350 or 619-596-7979.

Adzuki beans: A wonderful bean loaded with nutrients that is great when sprouted. Sprouting dramatically maximizes the vitamin and mineral content of this bean.

Almond butter (raw): Nut butter made from grinding almonds. This is a replacement for peanut butter as it is easier for the body to digest, and often there can be harmful toxins associated with peanut butter. Always buy raw and organic. Great in smoothies, on bread, or used in various recipes.

Basil: A wonderful aromatic herb that is better fresh but can also be used dried. With its distinct taste, this herb is perfect for pesto sauce. Commonly used in Italian dishes.

Bell peppers: A non-spicy variety of peppers often with a sweetness about them. Yellow, orange, and red are the varieties I use as the green ones are not ripe and do not digest as well. High in Vitamin C, these can be cut in strips and used to munch on throughout the day.

Celtic Sea Salt: The best form of salt to use, as it is hand harvested with rakes and then sundried. The only salt not refined or processed, containing approximately 80 natural occurring elements.

Cilantro: A parsley-like herb with a distinct taste commonly used in Mexican and Thai cuisine.

Coconut oil: Contains antibacterial, antiviral, anti-fungal properties. Abundant in medium chain fatty acids. Helps to improve HDL and LDL cholesterol ratios. Shown to support healthy thyroid function. Reduces hypoglycemic cravings. Great for skincare. Can withstand wide heat ranges without oxidation. Contains medium chain triglycerides (MCTs) which the body metabolizes quickly, converting the fats to energy rather than storing them as fat.

Coconut water and oil from young coconuts: The coconut has been called "the fluid of life" because it is a natural isotonic beverage, with the same level of electrolytic balance as we have in our blood. A great source of iron, potassium, vitamin C, natural sugars, and high in lauric oils. The medium-chain fats in coconut oil are similar to fats in mother's milk and have similar nutriceutical effects.

A study conducted in the Yucatan showed that those who used extra virgin coconut oil on a daily basis had a higher metabolic rate. The participants retained a lean body mass despite the fact that they regularly consumed considerable quantities of the saturated fat. In this same study it was noted that women participants did not suffer the typical symptoms of menopause.

Cumin: An age-old herb finely ground into a powder, known for its use in aiding digestion. Warm hearty flavor, used in Mexican and Indian cooking.

Curry: Recipes can vary depending on the ground spices used. Often containing cardamom, coriander, cumin, garlic, peppers and turmeric. A must for Indian cooking.

Dates: Derived from the date palm tree. My favorite variety is the medjool but khadrawi and honey also work well. Often used as a sweetener to replace sugar.

Dulse: A dark purply-red sea vegetable. Best to wash and even soak before use. Once dried, this seaweed can be ground into a coarse powder and sprinkled on food as one would salt.

Flaxseeds: A powerful seed with antioxidant properties, known to be especially helpful with breast cancer. Also a fabulous source of essential fatty acids and fiber. Can be ground and used in smoothies or sprinkled on salads. When soaked or used in liquids it turns quite gelatinous. Sometimes used as a thickener.

Garlic: The bulb of a plant in the amaryllis family, garlic has many wonderful properties. In the world of Italian cuisine, garlic is a staple. Fresh garlic is quite strong, so use the taste test before a heavy hand. Fresh garlic is a must in salsa.

Gamazio: Wonderful seasoning to sprinkle on food, made from Celtic Sea Salt and ground sesame seeds.

Ginger: Sold as a fresh root in the produce section near the fresh herbs or dried as a finely-ground powder. Store the root in the fridge, but watch out for mold after extended storage. Used to spice up many dishes. Ginger is a prime player in Asian cuisine. Great in salad dressings.

Honey: Made by bees from the nectar collected from flowers, this liquid sweetener should be used in its raw unfiltered state. Often sold by beekeepers at local farmer's markets. Contains enzymes and nutrients far superior to other sweeteners. Never give to babies under one year old, as they cannot digest it yet and it can be harmful for them.

Kelp: A wonderful seaweed. Also works as a great salt substitute when ground into a powder. Can be found in shaker containers in health food stores.

Kombu: My favorite sea vegetable. Great snipped into pieces and added to soups or to brown rice when cooking. Loaded with nutrients. (See *The Value of Sea Vegetables* for more information.)

Lemons: Can be used to replace vinegar in salad dressings. Also used to enhance and preserve food. Lemon juice will delay the oxidation process on avocados and apples that turns these fruits brown.

Nori: "Nori" is the Japanese name and "zicai" (purple vegetable) is the Chinese for a flat, blade-like red seaweed belonging to the genus Porphyra. The most popular sea vegetation used to make sushi, usually coming in flat sheets. Can be found in health food stores.

Nama Shoyu: Traditional unpasteurized soy sauce made from wheat. Alternative to regular soy sauce. Quite salty and not the best source of salt for the body, so use sparingly.

Parsley: A wonderful herb loaded with chlorophyll. Used to enhance recipes and often as a garnish.

Psyllium: A seed that is ground into a fine powder and often used to remedy constipation because of its high fiber content. When added to liquid it gels up. Used to help thicken recipes.

Pine nuts: Also known as pignolia, these soft white nuts come from pine cones. Great when used for sauces and dressings. Short shelf life, so it is best to store these in the freezer.

Raisins: Always buy unsulphured and organic to avoid harmful pesticides and chemicals. The best varieties for cooking are the Thompson or Monukka.

Scallions: Most commonly known as green onions. Great on salads or used as a condiment, as in a topping for baked potatoes.

Seaweeds: My favorite ones are arame, wakame, hijiki and kombu (see *The Value of Sea Vegetables* in the *RawSome Information* section for more info).

Sesame seeds: It is best to buy these delicate seeds unhulled to get maximum nutrients. These seeds are great sprinkled on stir fries. When ground up, they make a thick paste-like seed butter called Tahini.

Tahini: See sesame seeds. Always buy raw, organic and unsalted.

Udo's Choice Oil Blend: This oil is a wonderful blend of the Omega 3 and Omega 6 fatty acids made from organic flaxseeds, sunflower seeds and sesame seeds. In addition, wheat germ, oat germ and rye germ have been added to make this a well-rounded oil. Never heat. This oil can spoil easily so it is best to store in the freezer and never leave out for too long.

Vegenaise: My all time favorite mayonnaise, free of eggs, dairy and refined sweeteners. Made from grapeseed oil which is one of the "good" essential fatty acids.

Wakame: Also known as alaria, this seaweed comes in sheets and can be used to make sushi, crumpled up into flakes for soups or salads, or mixed in with grains.

Why Buy Locally Grown?

On every continent and in every climatic zone, people are realizing the benefits of buying local food. Usually picked just hours before market, produce found at local farmer's markets is fresher than anything in the supermarket. Ideally, the fresher the food, the more nutritious as well as delicious.

Another reason to shop at the local farmer's market is to support the local economy and bolster the small family farmers, enabling and encouraging them to continue their greatly needed and valued businesses.

Most importantly, we want to buy from and support the organic farmers who work so hard and have to jump through so many hurdles to be able to provide us with the best possible food.

For a reliable "living" public nationwide online directory of small farms, farmers markets, and other local food sources, type in **www.localharvest.org**. Local Harvest has a search engine to help people find local sources of sustainably grown food, and encourages them to establish direct contact with family farms in their local area.

For those of you in the Monterey Bay area, go to **www.montereybayfarmers.org** for information on our local organic farms and farmers markets, including times and directions to all the local markets.

Great Resources:

Anderson Almonds: Organic almonds by the case (25 lbs.) nice price reduction! 209-667-7494

Bariani Olive Oil: Unheated, unfiltered, stone-pressed organic olive oil. 916-689-9059

BellaVita Lifestyle Education Center: Residential 10 day cleanse, detox and rejuvenate program with a biblical diet base. Excellent comprehensive program emphasizing healing the whole person—body, mind and spirit. 800-655-3228 **www.modernmanna.org/bellavita_program.asp**

Big Tree Organics: Transitional almonds at great prices. 209-669-3678

California Certified Organic Farmers (CCOF): Toll free 888-423-2263 **www.ccof.org**

The Date People: Offering a huge selection of fresh organic dates. 760-359-3211

Diamond Organics: Offers beautiful organic produce including pastas, breads, wheatgrass and a wide range of organic products featured in their catalogue. No minimum purchase. Home delivery nationwide. Call for their catalog toll free 888-674-2642

The Fresh Network: World's most comprehensive raw and living foods organization, and publishers of Get Fresh! magazine. (UK phone number) +44(0)870-800-7070 **www.fresh-network.com**

GloryBee Foods, Inc.: Organic agave nectar and a range of other sweeteners and organic products. 541-689-0913 **www.glorybeefoods.com**

Grains of Salt: Celtic Sea Salt, toll free 800-867-7258. **www.celtic-seasalt.com**

Heintzman Farms: Purest source of organic gold flaxseeds. Toll free 888-333-5813. **www.Heintzmanfarms.com** or **www.flaxgold.com.**

Herbal Products and Development: Pacific Hemp Essential 7 Fine Oil Blend, 831-688-8706

Just Tomatoes: Great variety of dehydrated organic fruits and veggies. **www.justtomatoes.com**

Living Nutrition Magazine: Published biannually. 707-829-0362 **www.livingnutrition.com**

Optimum Health Institute: Reasonably priced retreat, healing and nutritional health resort teaching and providing raw living foods lifestyle. 800-993-4325 **www.optimumhealth.org**

Modern Manna Annual Health & Healing Crusade: Fantastic four-day event every June with nationally-acclaimed speakers, delicious vegetarian food and an expo featuring up to 100 exhibitors at Lodi's Grape Festival grounds (in CA).For more info, call 209-334-3868.

Platinum Health Products: Exceptional green products (kamut, spirulina, barley grass) at the fairest prices, as well as other high quality "super food" supplements. Toll free 888-747-6733 (referral code 1114) or **www.platinumhealthproducts.com/rawsome**

Pure Joy Living Foods: Living foods classes, the Amazing Nut-Milk Juice and Sprout Bag, mail order flax crackers, Raw/living foods books. **www.rawforlife.com, www.PureJoyLivingFoods.com**

RawSome Recipes: Best prices for all top-of-the-line juicers, dehydrators, blenders, spiral slicers and additional teflex sheets. Also, chemical-free beauty and household products as well as therapeutic-grade pure essential oils. E-mail your questions to: **wrboyd@earthlink.net** or **http://home.earthlink.net/~wrboyd**

Roxanne's Restaurant: "Now serving the community at the intersection of sensual flavors, healthy lifestyle and ecological sustainability..." Gourmet Raw food to live for! 320 Magnolia Avenue in Larkspur, California 415-924-5004

Sundance Country Farm: A bountiful selection from dried fruits and veggies to nut butters, bee pollen, herbs, spices, teas and much more. Toll free 888-269-9888

Swope Enterprises: Talk to Mary Ruth Swope, author of *Green Leaves of Barley* and *The Spiritual Roots of Barley* to order copies of her best selling books or discuss her research on barley grass. 903-562-1777

Tony's Italian Seasoning: Wonderful Italian herb seasoning without salt. 831-426-1235

Wholearth Spice: Great organic spice blends. 831-464-2409 or **www.wholearthspice.com**

Whole Food Farmacy: Wonderful products for both consumption and body care all made from 100% natural ingredients and whole foods.

Recommended Reading and Bibliography

1. Acciardo, Marcia *Light Eating for Survival*, Omango D'Press, Wethersfield CT, 1977
2. Balch, James and Phyllis, *Prescription for Nutritional Healing*, Avery Publishing Group, Garden City Park, NY, 1997
3. Bieler, Henry, M.D. *Food Is Your Best Medicine*, Ballantine Books, NY, 1965
4. Blaylock, Russell *Excitotoxins*, Health Press, Santa Fe, NM, 1997
5. Calabro, Rose Lee *Living in the Raw*, Rose Publishing, Santa Cruz, CA, 1998
6. Cousens, Gabriel, M.D. *Conscious Eating*, Essene Vision Books, Patagonia, AZ, 1992
7. Gottlieb, Bill *Alternative Cures*, Rodale Inc., 2000
8. Heller, Richard and Rachael *Carbohydrate Addicted Kids*, Harper Collins Publishers, NY, NY, 1997
9. Hovannessian, A.T. *Raw Eating*, Hallelujah Acres, Shelby, NC, reprint 2000
10. Malkmus, George *God's Way to Ultimate Health*, Hallelujah Acres,Shelby, NC, 1995
11. Malkmus, Rhonda *Recipes for Life*, Hallelujah Acres, Shelby, NC, 1998
12. Montgomery, Beth *Transitioning to Health: a Step by Step Guide for You and Your Child*, distributed by Nature's First Law, San Diego, CA, 2001
13. *Reader's Digest Foods That Harm, Foods That Heal*, Reader's Digest, Pleasantville, NY, 1997
14. Robbins, John *Diet for a New America*, Stillpoint Publishing, Walpole, NH, 1987
15. Shannon, Nomi *The Raw Gourmet*, Alive Books, Burnaby, BC, 1999
16. Swope, Mary, M.D. *Green Leaves of Barley*, Swope Enterprises, Lone Star, TX, 1987
17. Walker, Norman *Colon Health: the Key to a Vibrant Life*, Norwalk Press, 1979
18. Weimar Institute's *Newstart Lifestyle Cookbook,* Thomas Nelson Publishers, 1997
19. Wigmore, Ann *The Blending Book*, Avery Publishing Group, Garden City Park, NY, 1997
20. Yeager, Selene *The Doctors Book of Food Remedies*, Rodale Inc., 1998

About the Author

Robyn Boyd lives in Santa Cruz, CA with her husband, daughter, two cats and dog. She has been in the health care and fitness profession since 1977. She is a licensed and certified massage therapist.

Robyn has always had a passion for diet, nutrition and wellness. She owned and taught Work Your Buns Off aerobics fitness programs for eight years. Robyn also owned and directed Insight Body Works School of Massage in Eugene, Oregon.

Having fully recovered from Epstein Barr, Chronic Fatigue Syndrome, debilitating migraines and extreme hypoglycemia, Robyn speaks from experience. It is Robyn's passion to share the joy of living a healthy lifestyle with others. Her compassion and awareness of suffering help make her a teacher of depth. Robyn has also written a booklet (published by Rawsome Press) called *Health To Your Body, Nourishment To Your Bones* detailing her journey back to emotional, spiritual and physical health. In this booklet Robyn shares information that is both practical and spiritual.

Researching, writing and creating mouth-watering nutritious recipes are some of Robyn's passions. Robyn loves to travel and is available to speak or teach hands-on "uncooking" workshops whenever her schedule permits.

Pepper painting by Robyn's daughter, Molly (age 12).
Back cover photo of Robyn Boyd by Lloyd Tabb

Index of Recipes

Index

Acid: 7, 10, 17, 24, 27-28, 35-36, 41, 46, 63
Acidosis: 24
A.D.D.: 47
ADHD: 47-48
Adzuki Beans: 25, 37, 46, 99, 173
Agave: 13-14, 28, 70-71, 80, 85, 88-89, 95, 107, 112, 117, 129, 136, 149, 154, 156-157, 169, 173, 176
Alcohol: 20, 25, 47-48
Algae:: 20
Alkaline: 7, 24-25, 36
Alkalinity: 24-25
Allergies: 27-28, 48
Almonds: 11, 13-15, 21-23, 25, 45-46, 49, 53, 55-61, 67, 69, 72, 75, 77-81, 87, 89, 91, 96, 105-106, 112, 114, 116-118, 121, 125, 129-130, 136-137, 139, 141, 143-146, 149-157, 163-164, 167-171, 173, 176, 181-183
Almonnaise: 75, 91, 168, 181
Amaranth: 19
Apples: 12, 14, 19, 25, 28, 33, 40, 53, 55-57, 60, 62, 82, 91, 141, 143, 155, 157, 163-164, 167-168, 175, 181-182
Applesauce: 112, 141, 143, 146, 156, 182
Apricots: 14, 28, 40, 46, 49, 55, 57, 63, 77, 80, 88-89, 108, 111, 116, 123, 126, 141, 143, 163, 166, 182
Arame: 21, 75, 90, 175, 181
Artichokes: 19, 40
Asparagus: 40, 46, 93, 96, 103, 116, 121, 139, 165, 181-182
Aspartame: 10, 28
Avocados: 14, 25, 27, 40, 49, 65, 67-68, 70, 72, 80-82, 84-85, 87-88, 91, 95-96, 101, 105, 107, 110, 113, 133-134, 150, 153-154, 164, 175, 181
B-Vitamins: 16, 18-19, 28, 41
Bacteria: 19-20, 28, 48, 171-172
Bananas: 14, 27, 40, 45-46, 53, 56-61, 67, 72-73, 141, 144, 147, 150-156, 163-164, 166-167, 171, 181-182
Barley: 14, 16, 20, 23, 25-26, 29, 33, 46, 53, 58, 62, 93, 98, 118, 164, 170, 177-178, 181
Basil: 70, 81, 84, 88, 95, 108, 111, 115, 118, 121, 124, 138, 166, 173, 182
Beans: 14, 21-23, 25, 37, 40-41, 46, 49, 75, 87-88, 93, 97-99, 101, 103, 106, 113-114, 119, 121, 132, 138, 151, 165, 173, 181-182

Bee Pollen: 16, 20, 177
Beet Greens: 40
Beets: 40, 84, 97, 105
Bell Peppers: ii, 27, 69, 75, 78, 80-82, 84-85, 95, 101, 106-107, 109, 126, 128-129, 131, 135, 170, 173, 181
Berries: 27, 56, 58, 63, 153, 155-156, 163, 166
Beta-carotene: 19, 40-42, 57
Blackberries: 40, 56, 150-151, 153
Blood Glucose: 31-32
Blood pH: 24
Blood Sugar: 32
Blueberries: 40, 56, 63, 150, 153-154, 167
Bok Choy: 106
Bread: 13, 45, 72, 103, 112, 132, 136, 138, 141, 164-165, 167, 173, 182
Brewer's yeast: 16, 20, 33, 60, 164, 171
Broccoli: 23, 27, 40, 46, 67, 75, 77, 85, 87, 106, 114, 117, 168, 181
Brussels Sprouts: 40
Buckwheat: 25, 40, 56, 84, 107, 121, 135, 182
Butter: 11, 14, 17-18, 25, 45-47, 56, 60-61, 67, 72-73, 82, 97-98, 100, 107, 112, 115, 117-119, 121, 136, 144, 146, 149, 155-157, 165, 173, 175, 182
Butternut Squash: 23, 103, 118, 182
Cabbage: 40, 79, 84-85, 89, 97, 103, 105, 117, 164-165, 167, 182
Cadmium: 17
Caffeine: 11, 44, 47, 49, 169
Calcium: 7, 19, 21-24, 40-42, 46, 49, 99
Cancer: 3, 7, 16, 18-19, 23-26, 28, 38, 40, 42, 57, 174
Canned Foods: 13-14
Carbohydrates: 17, 21, 29, 32-34, 36, 45, 48-49, 178
Carob: 14, 19-20, 29, 49, 58-59, 141, 145, 149-150, 152-153, 163-164, 167, 170, 182
Carrots: 16, 25, 27, 40, 62, 67, 70-72, 77, 79, 89, 98-99, 101, 105-107, 110, 113, 117, 119, 129, 141, 145, 164, 170, 182
Cashews: 14, 68, 75, 80, 85, 87, 103, 108-109, 121, 126, 143, 146, 164-165, 167-168, 181-182
Cauliflower: 27, 40, 77, 87, 103, 118-119, 168, 182
Celery: 27, 39-40, 46, 62, 67, 69, 72, 77, 79, 81-82, 84, 88-89, 91-92, 96-99, 119, 129, 170

Cellulite: 33
Celtic Sea Salt: 13, 14, 37, 39, 71, 72, 73, 77, 78, 79, 81, 82, 89, 91, 95, 96, 97, 99, 108, 110, 112, 114, 115, 117, 130, 131, 132, 136, 138, 139, 174, 177
Chai: 53, 61, 181
Chard: 27, 115
Cheese: 12-13, 25, 46, 78, 82, 87, 111, 113, 115, 117, 124, 164, 166, 169
Cherries: 40
Chia: 19
Children: 5, 17, 23, 45-48, 51, 109
Chilies: 85, 133
Chlorella: 16-17
Chlorophyll: 16, 20-21, 175
Cholesterol: 17-19, 23, 28, 40, 57, 174
Chromium: 16, 33, 49
Cilantro: 69-71, 81, 85, 89-90, 96-97, 105, 107, 129, 133-134, 137-138, 174
Cinnamon: 14, 55-57, 59, 100-101, 136, 143-146, 149, 153, 155-156, 163, 171-172
Citrus: 27
Cloves: 71, 77-78, 80-82, 85, 89, 97-98, 100-101, 107, 111, 115-117, 124-126, 128-129, 132-134, 136, 138-139
Coconuts: 11, 13-14, 18, 40, 53, 55, 59, 61-62, 67, 93, 95-96, 121, 123-124, 136-137, 141, 143-146, 149-152, 154, 157, 159, 166-168, 174, 181-182
Coffee: 13, 15, 18, 20, 130, 134, 149, 156
Collard Greens: 46
Collards: 23, 27, 99, 115
Corn: 48, 68, 75, 81, 85, 88, 103, 112, 115, 121, 128-130, 133, 167, 181-182
Couscous: 14
Cranberries: 25, 40, 75, 85, 91, 168, 181
Cucumbers: 27, 40, 62, 65, 67, 70, 75, 77-78, 81-82, 84, 88-89, 93, 96, 121, 123, 125, 170, 181-182
Cumin: 14, 37, 77, 80, 99, 118, 129, 174
Currants: 14, 40, 79-80, 101, 114, 144-146, 149, 155
Curry: 14, 75, 80, 93, 96, 100, 129, 174, 181
Dates: 5, 13, 28, 40, 45, 56, 59, 61, 78-80, 91, 108, 111, 123, 126, 129, 143-147, 149-154, 156-157, 159, 163, 167, 169, 174, 176
DDT: 17
Diabetes: 7, 23, 28-32
Dill: 14, 79, 98

RawSome Recipes Workshops

Hands-on, in the kitchen, un-cooking workshops, created by Robyn Boyd. Workshops are held monthly—for current schedule, email **wrboyd@earthlink.net**. Classes are also listed at: **http://home.earthlink.net/~wrboyd**.

In this class, you'll learn how to:

- Make life-supporting and disease-resisting RawSome breakfasts, lunches, and dinners

- Create wheatgrass cocktails, fabulous breakfast smoothies, raw oatmeal with papaya pudding, homemade almond milk, solar tacos, great mock tuna salad, angel hair pasta out of zucchini, dairy-free mango ice cream and other wonderful surprises!

- Also learn:
  - how and why to incorporate green foods
  - what are the good oils
  - how to get enough quality protein / recipes that kids will enjoy
  - traveling tips
  - great kitchen equipment and chemical free products for home and personal use
  - how to transition a step at a time

- Make over a dozen delicious recipes from the *RawSome Recipes* cookbook and try them all! Bring your heartiest appetite!

What people are saying:

"This was a very informative and helpful workshop. It was a great way to learn rather than just reading about it." – Dr. Cathy Petronijevic

"Robyn is very knowledgeable—a real expert. This day was lots of fun!" – Michelle Waters, author of *Dancing With The Diagnosis*

"This was very informative, nutritious and delicious—very gourmet and beyond my expectations! I highly recommend this, even you are not a vegetarian, to supplement your diet with wholesome, fresh-tasting food." – Kathy Burt, graduate of the Culinary Institute

"Excellent, inspiring instruction, beautiful setting, delicious, scrumptious recipes for every meal." – Patti Mills, publisher of *The Connection* magazine

"Fabulous - a 'must do' for anyone who wants to increase their repertoire. Robyn does a fantastic job of providing nutritional wisdom and hands on information." – Janet Fine

"This class will change your life and your health" – Richard Maestas

"The food we make in this class is the best I ever tasted and made!" – Jenny Anne Lukan, Age 10

To order additional books, contact Essential Science Publishing at:
www.essentialscience.net or call **800-336-6308**

Notes: